the big difference

I'M DOING RATHER

WHAT I'D BE DOING

the big difference

life works when you choose it

Nicola Phillips

PERSEUS
PUBLISHING
A Member of the
Perseus Books Group

www.yourmomentum.com

the stuff that drives you

What is momentum?

Momentum is a completely new publishing philosophy, in print and online, dedicated to giving you more of the information, inspiration and drive to enhance who you are, what you do, and how you do it.

Fusing the changing forces of work, life and technology, momentum will give you the bright stuff for a brighter future and set you on the way to being all you can be.

Who needs momentum?

Momentum is for people who want to make things happen in their career and their life, who want to work at something they enjoy and that's worthy of their talent and their time. Momentum people have values and principles, and question who they are, what they do, and who for. Wherever they work, they want to feel proud of what they do. And they are hungry for information, stimulation, ideas and answers …

Momentum online

Visit www.yourmomentum.com to be part of the talent community. Here you'll find a full listing of current and future books, an archive of articles by momentum authors, sample chapters and self-assessment tools. While you're there, post your worklife questions to our momentum coaches and sign up to receive free newsletters with even more stuff to drive you

More momentum

If you need more drive for your life, try one of these titles, all published under the momentum label:

change activist
make big things happen fast
Carmel McConnell

lead yourself
be where others will follow
Mick Cope

happy mondays
putting the pleasure back into work
Richard Reeves

hey you!
pitch to win in an ideas economy
Will Murray

snap, crackle or stop
change your career and create your own destiny
Barbara Quinn

float you
how to capitalize on your talent
Carmel McConnell & Mick Cope

innervation
rewire yourself for a smarter future
Guy Browning

coach yourself
make real change in your life
Tony Grant & Jane Greene

from here to e
equip yourself for a career in the wired economy
Lisa Khoo

grow your personal capital
what you know, who you know and how you use it
Hilarie Owen

Many of the designations used by manufacturers and sellers to distinguish their products are claimed as trademarks. Where those designations appear in this book and Perseus Publishing was aware of a trademark claim, the designations have been printed in initial capital letters.

Copyright © Pearson Education Limited 2001

This edition of *The Big Difference: life works when you choose it* First Edition is published by arrangement with Pearson Education Limited.

Library of Congress Cataloging-in-Publication Data is available.
ISBN 0-7382-0654-7

Perseus Publishing is a member of the Perseus Books Group.

Find us on the World Wide Web at http://www.perseuspublishing.com

Perseus Publishing books are available at special discounts for bulk purchases in the U.S. by corporations, institutions, and other organizations. For more information, please contact the Special Markets Department at the Perseus Books Group, 11 Cambridge Center, Cambridge, MA 02142, or call (800) 255-1514 or (617) 252-5298, or e-mail j.mccrary@perseusbooks.com.

Text design by George Hammond, Diss, Norfolk

First printing, August 2002

1 2 3 4 5 6 7 8 9 10 – 03 02 01

about the author . . .

Nicola Phillips has been a coach, consultant and author on innovation and change since 1981, in Europe, the US and the Middle and Far East. Her assignments include projects in the media, finance, commercial, information technology, production and public sectors. She has an executive coaching practice which deals with work and personal issues ranging from mentoring executives and directors to designing new processes for e-business. She has written *E-motional Business*, *Reality Hacking*, *Managing International Teams*, *Innovative Management* and *Motivating Through Change*. She is currently doing what she would rather be doing in Santa Cruz, California.

acknowledgments . . .

Hilary and Paddy for provocation both oral and intellectual. And paper and coffee.

Dee and Al for giving with forgetting.

KT and Laura for the stuff no one else says.

Susan for putting body into soul.

SS for warmth, ecru and tidiness.

Nick and his sensei for muse capacity.

BigRazbird . . . for being brave and fearless in the face of paper and bolshi women.

Don't let the papers fall out of the cupboard.

Richard; what can one say when you run out of superlatives? Nothing. There's a first.

Lauren for everything.

Redheads do what blondes dream about . . .
I am doing what I'd rather be doing . . .

choosing and losing

the story so far ...

take no notice of the man behind the curtain ...

stuck

living in chaotic space

f8 and be there

the big difference

It is extraordinarily hard to know what you want.

It is harder in a way to know what you want than how to get it.
Sometimes we block our desires for fear we won't get them. Our
fears of disappointment and rejection are so huge that we will stay
with things we are unhappy with because we know them. Fear of the
unknown is so big.

I like big. It's a good word. Short but expansive.

It makes me smile when I say it.

Choosing what you want is the biggest difference you can make in
your life.

You cannot be doing what you'd rather be doing until you have
made that choice. Not the decision, an informed choice. Choice about
what you are, what you want and what you will have to lose to do it.

In every aspect of life we find ourselves in situations that we did not
choose, discovering attitudes and perspectives we didn't know we
had, feeling forced to stick to decisions which we only later realize
that we ourselves had made. Sometimes we refuse to accept the

situation; other times, we surrender with grace. Each time we have to struggle with our desire for everything to be ok, and/or for someone to do it for us.

The thought that someone out there must know the answer, if only I knew who I could copy them, is extremely attractive.

Balance. Horrid word. Doesn't make me grin.

One of those things we are supposed to have in our lives or at least strive for. What constitutes a balance is hard to gauge. For me it is probably not so much about balance as about appropriateness. Balance seems to imply that there is a right and wrong measure for the number of different things you do. I am not convinced of this, but I can see how being aware of what is appropriate allows you to be free enough to choose what actions you might take. Whether you take the option on that freedom, and are ready to be accountable for being free, is another story.

This is not intended to be a deep, conceptual, philosophical book. It is meant to provoke thoughts not answers. Once you have the thoughts, the answers come. If someone else gives you answers, they are not yours; they haven't come from your thoughts.

People tend to do things out of fear or incentive. Doing things out of fear gets us doing stuff, but anything born out of fear is not a choice, it's a decision. We don't commit to things we do out of fear. The best we can hope for is resentful compliance.

So part of the decision comes down to understanding what would be in it for you to go through this struggle.

Understanding how luck figures in the equation, as opposed to seizing opportunities, is part of solving the puzzle of doing what you'd rather be doing. Knowing what an opportunity looks like and how that differs from a fatalistic approach helps the decision process.

That only comes with a desire to be open and take risks.

That only comes with a desire for questions rather than answers.

Your curiosity and intrigue need to be as important to you as your emotional and intellectual experiences. If not, you end up suffering from experiential myopia, where your only view of the world is based on what you think you already know, with no space for anything else. If you do what you have always done, you will get what you have always got...

The world tells you that you make your life happen, your life doesn't make you happen. I disagree. The two can be the same thing. Most of us compose our lives around what happens. Life isn't static, but throws up all sorts of opportunities to think, feel and respond differently. Changes in circumstances or situations themselves do not necessarily make us change. It is our response to the situations that creates change in ourselves.

This isn't about predicting what might happen or consciously structuring out or mapping your future. It is to do with knowing your past, understanding your present, living your present, and the future becomes the future, not a goal.

(It does make choosing what flavour ice cream you want a breeze.)

Everything works. Nothing works for very long.

It takes time to become acquainted with yourself. You get built and added to every day of your life, but we rarely take time out to see the construction. You are often not even the architect. Great architects will ask questions about the things that you value in your life, and about the things that are important to you.

We rarely take the time to ask ourselves those questions.

To take risks and reach new shores means having a vessel to come back to. So knowing that vessel well is fundamental to an ability to move on.

There are times in our lives when it is impossible to see what is happening because we have no point of reference, or are too embroiled to get perspectives. It is not possible to make choices at these times because we are blind.

We tend to take decisions or drift. It doesn't mean that we cannot use the experience in a later story development, or that our responses are "wrong" (whatever that means).

Understanding how to observe ourselves and the stories of our lives is at the heart of the choosing process. If we cannot see who we are, we don't know what we are dealing with. This means knowing what to look for.

This book may not give you answers, but its intention is to show you where you might look to find them.

It is all in the Awareness, Honesty and Acceptance. Huge words. That for me is what an AHA is.

Easily said, the most difficult things to actually achieve.

Even the acknowledged act of standing still and looking around is a step forward.

This book is about looking around you and seeing what is there.

So let's get to the difficult bit: how we find out what matters to us.

It begins with the questions…

The questions we ask change the world we see.

"always a more beautiful
answer that asks a
more beautiful question."

e.e. cummings

How do we keep the momentum of mind, body, and spirit?

Where does the energy and motivation come from?

How do other people figure in our stories, decisions and choices?

How do I balance analysis and emotion?

How can I know what I want?

How can I know what I don't want?

How can I know what I don't know?

How can I know what questions to ask?

So many questions. Maybe too many. So overwhelming. Much easier to just go along with whatever the slings and arrows throw at you and whine about it. Provoking thought is always a risky business, as it raises the level of awareness of what you don't have. If that is a discomfort you would rather not experience, stop reading. On the other hand, that level of discomfort may be nowhere near as bad as you think it might be. (Notice how many variables were in that sentence; doing what you would rather be doing is about experiencing variables.)

"Supposing a tree fell down, Pooh, when we were underneath it?"
"Supposing it didn't," said Pooh.
After careful thought Piglet was comforted by this.

A.A. Milne

So if you choose to take up the challenge of making the big difference, this book is about setting you on the road. You have to take the steering wheel and drive. The book is separated into sections which may or may not be read sequentially. It may be hard to understand what doing things differently would be like if you haven't had the opportunity to understand what lies behind it. On the other hand, there is no reason why you couldn't read a section twice…it would be unusual to gain nothing from reinforcement ……

Choosing and losing	Choices: What is a choice? Why is it so hard?
The story so far …	Me: Who am I? What is my story?
Take no notice of the man behind the curtain	Fantasy, illusion: How do I tell fantasy from reality? What's the impact of the illusion?
Stuck	Fears and prisons: Why am I drawn to this? Why do I feel so stuck?
Living in chaotic space	Risk and ambiguity: Why is not knowing so hard? What would it take to move me?
F8 and be there	Making the big difference: How can I/do I live it?
Let's go.	

"Now watch the tree
that sheds its life
and you will see
the leaves of change
will always fall
but the tree itself
remains."

David Streeter

choosing and losing

"ALL ORGANISMS WITH COMPLEX NERVOUS SYSTEMS ARE FACED WITH THE MOMENT BY MOMENT QUESTION THAT IS POSED BY LIFE:

WHAT SHALL I DO NEXT?"

Sue Savage Rumaugh and Roger Lewin

choosing and losing

So how do you get to do what you'd rather be doing, and why is it
you think there may be something else you would rather be doing?

Numerous media constantly exhort that you always have a choice.
You may always have one, but you don't always take one.

Making a choice involves knowing what we want, before we can
choose what to do next. If we do not know that, life becomes a series
of actions without fulfilment. Deciding what to do next in a vacuum
usually leaves us feeling dissatisfied.

Why did you take the job that you have – or get married, or go to
college, or take some advanced training? There would of course be
specific reasons you would give for each of these decisions, but you
probably have not thought about a powerful thread that runs
through every decision in your life and lies at the basis of everything
that all of us do.

Choosing.

What is choice? Do we always have it?

Free will. Is it the same thing?

For you to see you have a choice, you have to be aware of the meaning you attach to it.

"If you want to identify me, ask me not where I live, or what I like to eat, or how I comb my hair, but ask me what I am living for, in detail, and ask me what I think is keeping me from living fully for the thing I want to live for."

Thomas Merton

The definition of us is the thing we want to live for. At different times in our lives it may be different things, but usually an underlying value, known or otherwise, will shape our ends, rough hew them how we may. We are usually at the happiest moments in our lives when that value is being met. It could be something like freedom, creating something, or being cared for.

It is less likely to be the things we often wish for, such as money, good health, a promotion, a child. These are really manifestations of the things that are of value. Sometimes that indefinable feeling of wind in your hair and the sun shining on you just makes you grin uncontrollably. Are these things we can choose, or are what we need to be able to choose the opportunities that will enable us to experience and have those things?

"Je ne sais peut-etre pas ce que je veux
mais je sais ce que je ne veux pas."

Samie Farah

We rarely know what we want, but we often think we know what we don't want. Even then, it is often hard to articulate it as a potential choice.

We don't know what we don't know, but when you are open enough to see it, it becomes a possibility. Not knowing is often so scary that we have to shut down and say there is nothing else.

We very rarely know nothing. It's just that what we do know seems confused and without any clarity. Is there a way we can make more conscious some of the ideas that flash through, but get dismissed as not being concrete enough? If we can maintain our gaze on new things for long enough, new things evolve. When you look again, you see more possibilities. It is almost like turning over the soil to aerate it. It is the same piece of soil, seen from another angle. Sometimes the truth we seek is lurking, waiting for us to have the guts to see it. Not knowing is a strange state of mind, but it doesn't mean we have no answers. It means we don't know, and there is a process we have to go through to change that state of mind.

"In these times I don't, in a manner of speaking, know what I want; perhaps I don't want what I know and want what I don't know."

Marsilio Ficino

Why on earth do we expect to know what we want? So hard to distinguish between needs and wants, and sometimes one becomes the other. It is harder to say what you want than what you need; what you want is way more personal. Saying what you need is almost verging on the practical and therefore justifiable. Maybe saying what you want is hard, for fear ...

That you might get it ...

That you might not get it ...

It's not true ...

It is true.

choosing and losing

the big difference

momentum

"I don't know what sort of world she will live in and I have no fixed opinions concerning how she should live in it. I only know that if she does not come to value what is true above what is useful it will make little difference whether she lives at all. And by true I do not mean what is righteous, but merely what is so."

Cormac McCarthy

Children know what they want in that moment, but have no interest in knowing why it is important to them. Indeed, why would they need to know? As grown-ups, we often miss the beauty of doing something in the moment because it is what we want, and feel the need to justify it and rationalize it – even to the point of criticizing others we see doing things because they want to. This isn't about totally selfish living, although it could be. It's about understanding how we often do know what it is we would rather be doing, but we bury it under all sorts of disguises.

Sarah leaned forward in her chair and sipped her coffee tentatively. She replaced it on the table, and glanced around the room. She fiddled with the zip on her sweatshirt, and then huddled herself further inside it. Her hands were hidden inside the sleeves and her shoulders were hunched.

"Why does everyone expect me to choose what I want? I don't know and don't know how to know. The more people ask, the more nervous I become. I feel as though I am letting people down by not knowing.

"I look around and they don't seem to know what they want, but they expect me to. It's almost as if I have to know so they feel better about themselves not knowing. Maybe if I don't know they feel obliged to find an answer. No one must be allowed to wander around ..."

She smiled wryly and leaned back. Sarah's story is of an articulate woman in her mid-twenties who has always seemed more focused than she is. She had been successful at school and university, then had a job with an advertising agency, and gave it up to go and work overseas as an English teacher in Africa. She enjoyed her year abroad, and one year after her return still has not settled. She doesn't miss Africa, or even the work, but knows she feels dissatisfied. If you ask her why she went to Africa, she says she just wanted to get out of the rat race, and do something that directly benefited another human being. Ask her why that was important, and she has no answer. Ask why that moment in time, and she has no answer. She went in search of something, but didn't know what. That was probably less important to know than why she needed to search.

We spend time worrying about what we want to do, without thinking about why what we are doing currently is unsatisfactory.

What tells us we are at a choice point?

Sammy turned around, her eyes sparking. "Maybe I have never made a choice in my life. That is scary. My mother chose my college, my friends chose my first husband, and I ended up in the career that I have because I love performing. It's a drug. But I never actually chose it. Now that I am trying to make a change in my life, I am finding it very hard to decide what is important. I don't seem able to find my voice. I can find it for everyone else, but not for me. I don't think I am willing to let go of anything. I want it all. Is that because I don't want to choose? Why wouldn't I want to?"

Sammy is an extremely confident, successful executive. That doesn't stop her having difficulty making a choice. She even has a pretty clear idea of what is important to her. The bit that is missing is her ability to let go of something.

Making a choice not only means knowing what you want, it also means knowing what you will lose when you make a choice, and accepting the loss.

Frequently that is the hardest thing to accept.

"A threat of loss creates anxiety, and actual loss, sorrow; both, moreover, are likely to arouse anger."

John Bowlby

Most people never get past the anxiety state in terms of changing their behaviour. That state is so difficult that it paralyzes them, stops them from doing anything. The anger shows in the subsequent frustration. One theory suggests that it is the duality of a decision that is scary. We see things in terms of two options only: you will be either one or the other. For example, you are either good or bad.

In this polarity, you identify with one or the other, and fear that you might become the one you have not identified with: fat/thin, good/evil. Certainly the idea of extremes is very likely to incur a higher level of anxiety than some vagueness. It is worth considering that before you set yourself up for extremes.

"All happy families are alike, but each unhappy family is unhappy in its own way."

Tolstoy

Maybe the first question to ask is, what drives us? What gets us out of bed in the morning? If you can't answer that question in general, can you answer it for specific situations? For example, if I asked you what gets you out of bed in the morning when you are on holiday, would you have a clearer answer? If you have, you may be beginning to see my point. (Alternatively, nothing may get you out of bed on holiday.) It may not be the actual "thing" that gets you out of bed that is important; it is what is important to you about that thing. What is it that doing that "thing" will give you? What is the drive and need behind doing the "thing"? If we all have drives and needs, they are drives and needs in order to...?

This seems to me to be a bigger question than analyzing needs. If what you want is to be happy, then you can begin to look at what would make you happy. If you want to stay miserable, or are scared to be happy in case someone takes it away, then your needs are likely to be very different.

Sammy said she loved performing, but on being asked what she loved about it, she couldn't articulate it.

So the **BIG** question is not what would make me happy, but what do I want in life?

Without that general direction, it's hard to know what would help you get there. You might say, well everyone wants to be happy, but do they? And what does happy mean for us?

There seem to be three key drivers: Self-belief, Belonging and Control. It is the interaction of these which really creates the choice points for us. None of them is more or less important, although you could argue that self-belief governs what you feel in terms of control, and your relationship needs. You could also argue the converse; that your level of control need and need to belong create your self-belief.

The powerhouse in any story is the will of the characters to get or do what matters to them. So they need to know what matters; it needs to matter enough that they are prepared to work for it, and they need to understand what it would take to get what they want.

Self-belief

"Two opposing drives operate throughout life: the drive for companionship, love, and everything else which brings us close to our fellow men; and the drive toward being independent, separate, and autonomous."

Anthony Storr

This is about the things we achieve strictly through our own actions. The things which drive us through doing something ourselves; not for any external validation, but for an internal personal sense of self-fulfilment.

◆ **Need for autonomy:** doing things the way you want to do them, without anyone looking over your shoulder.

◆ **Creativity:** doing something new or in a new way.

◆ **Personal growth:** continuously learning.

Rob kept ruffling the papers on his clipboard. He had just completed a restructure of his department, and he had no job in the brave new world. He had hidden behind the details of the restructure, but was now having to face up to his decisions. He spoke abruptly as though if he spoke the words quickly, they might disappear.

"I can't think about the future. I'm unwilling to think about the future. On the other hand, I can't not do it. The future is being pushed on me. I'm not even sure what decision I have to make. I can't decide, I don't know what there is to choose from. I don't really feel as though I have a constant. It's hard to feel safe without a constant. Sometimes I just want to run away. If I deal with the immediate problem of there not being a job for me, then I miss dealing with the big picture about what I want. Do I deal with the presenting problem or the real one? Having said that, I am not sure I know what the real one is. **Now** is too in my face."

He had always had a sense of autonomy, but within a highly structured world. In the future, there would be far more ambiguity for him in any job he took. Taking away the structure had taken away large chunks of his self-confidence.

Belonging

Feeling accepted.

Feeling a part of something.

Feeling valued and appreciated.

"Most people, especially highly gifted people, do not really know where they belong until they are well past their mid-twenties. By that time, however, they should know the answers to the three questions: What are my strengths? How do I perform? and What are my values? And then they can and should decide where they belong."

Peter Drucker

A producer summed up this conflict in him by saying that he had always regarded himself as a loner, but he was at his most productive when around large groups of people. His whole experience was about shared experience. He said that if he was in a forest by himself, there was no forest.

Life as we know it is for most of us not just our story. We interact with people every day, friends, colleagues, strangers. Every interaction brings with it new possibilities or re-runs of old ones. It is often easier for us to be carried along by other people's stories and expectations than to keep to our own stories. **WHY**?

We can never know for sure whether or not people see things the way we do. What proportion of people are privately disenchanted with the beliefs they publicly affirm? How many stand alone because they do not know how to join the group?

"What other people think of you is none of your......business."

Sheldon Kopp

Control

Feeling safe in your environment.

Knowing your boundaries.

This is not about control of others, although it might end up that way. It is more about remaining safe. One way to do that is to master a skill so that you feel competent in it. Competence gives you confidence. This demands practice and commitment. This is played out by many in terms of their perceived devotion to work. If I work all these hours, I will get better. Do you define your work or does it define you? If your work was taken away, would you feel your identity had gone with it? Did you choose it?

Interestingly enough my observation of people is that they feel more regret at the things they did *not* try, than the things they did try that didn't work out. I can almost see you nod your heads at this. So why is it so hard to take the risk? (If I keep asking you the question, maybe you'll appreciate the fact that the bigger risk lies in doing nothing...) Nothing in life is ever finished, so why expect it? If life is an ongoing work in progress, then trying something is part of the work in progress. No one knows when their deadline is going to appear, so

why treat life like a timed, focused work project?

It isn't. It's life.

Everything we "know" is an approximation; nothing is exact. Why is it then we search for the "right" thing, feeling it to be something clearly defined and focused? We can only focus on what we know well, so things which are unfamiliar to us we tend to push to the side of our vision or block them out altogether. That way we feel we are in some way "controlling" our lives.

When the body is not trying too hard, the mind can respond. Maybe that's the other way round; when the mind is not trying too hard, the body can respond. If we include the heart and soul as autonomous parts of the body, limbic rather than neuro-cortical, maybe we get in touch with more....

The inner game is subtraction, not addition.

It's time to try to ground some of these concepts in you. Looking at yourself in terms of these three categories – self-belief, belonging and control. Which carries the most weight for you?

How do you think you behave in relation to these categories?

Is there one that you would choose if you could have only one?

Try not to explore for solutions, just explore....

Great expectations

We often confuse expectations with desires and wants. What we expect may come from what we want; it may also come from what we fear. The fear may not just be of something "bad", such as "failure", it may also be of something that was nominally "good", such as success.

Bruce Sterling has a bracing requirement for organizations he works with. He tells them: "Imagine the victory condition for your organization." He then helps them imagine it, and asks: "Do you think you could bear it?" For many organizations, it's more than they can bear.

If we have expectations, we have not necessarily made a choice; in fact, it is very unlikely.

"In addition to the chance blows to which life subjects everyone else, we add the needless suffering that comes from impossible demands that we be special, and that the world be fair and just."

Sheldon Kopp

These expectations are often closely linked with a sense of nostalgia for a past that may or may not have happened. We often hope for a future that will be better without looking at what "better" means. We often fritter away our lives waiting for a happy ending or some deus ex-machina to deliver "the" solution. The comforting illusions of the past often distort our desires and expectations for the future.

Even if the past wasn't that great, because it was then and it has already happened, it invokes some feeling of safety that allows us to say past good, future bad. Our past has relevance for us, but it is not necessarily our future.

> "The human spirit may crave freedom but it recoils from choice..."
>
> Andrew Anthony

Marx suggested that men make their own destinies, but not in circumstances of their own choosing. How we interpret and make sense of the events that happen is the key to our ability and desire to choose.

To understand ourselves we have to know our story; to know our story we have to understand ourselves....

This could also be described variously as "making the best out of a bad job", "dealing with whatever comes my way", "responding to what is happening". For me these comments underline the difference between a choice and a decision.

A decision is when you decide to do something you feel you need, ought or should do. The decision may have no basis in data or it may have lots. It is usually based around an action you think needs to happen.

A choice is more to do with an understanding of you in the situation. It is often a much more systemic thought process, affecting more than one aspect of our lives. It frequently revolves around what issues are important, rather than actions that need to be taken.

> "Neither either or – always both and."
>
> Jean Houston

When you make a choice, you know what you want (not need). You know what it will take. You know what you will lose and what that will cost.

Most importantly of all, you accept the implications of choosing. That is, you accept that what you do will bring something, and whatever that something is, you will be comfortable with it. This is really tough. It means

you are the only one responsible and accountable for what happens

(including how you deal with any intervention by the slings and arrows of outrageous fortune).

No wonder we rarely make choices; we often drift into things or say, "I might as well" or "here goes". These are decisions, not choices. They do not leave you free. Only a choice makes you free.

Freedom has the cost of accountability attached to it. Decisions don't come with the power to enforce them. Power comes with choice.

Are you ready, accepting and grounded enough to do that?

Freedom is accountability.

It's *mine. I* did it.

CHOICE	DECISION
I want	I need to
	I ought, should
I feel and think	I think
I am happy, content	Restless, maybe I could have, if only
I have lost . . .	I still have to
I know what has happened	"What if . . ."
Don't need to keep looking back	Keep rehashing what has happened
Acceptance	Knowledge
Yes and	Yes but

It's really, really, really hard to make a choice.

Think about your life.

Based on these criteria, you can probably count on one hand the number of choices you have made in your life. School, university, job, relationship, children – all the big so-called choices – have probably been made for you or have been decisions. The real choices you have made will have left you feeling content, no matter what outcome they had. They are also likely to be points in your life where you really felt you had changed. The difference explains why we think we have made choices but have in fact taken decisions, and then wonder why we are still wanting ...

The Rolling Stones have a slightly different take on it:

"You can't always get what you want,
but if you try sometimes,
you just might find
you get what you need."

Many say they accept what has happened; what they really mean is they know what has happened; they don't necessarily accept it. Speculation is so much safer than finding out the truth.

Chris Argyris suggests that the more data you have about your environment, the more choice you have. Jim March suggests that it doesn't matter how much data you have: risk will always be a determining and unpredictable variable of any choice.

"The heart has its reasons whereof Reason knows nothing."

Pascal

When you ask yourself, why is it so hard to make a choice and be free, it's worth asking, why would I want to be free?

"Do you wanna go for a ride?"

"Hell, yes!"

A choice is about doing the right thing. A decision is about doing something right.

How do you know what you want? Your choices are only as good as your requests ...

Antonio Damasio suggests that the purpose of reasoning when you are deciding is selecting a response to a given situation; that is an action, sentence or a combination of what seems possible in the particular circumstances. Reasoning and deciding are so interwoven that they are often used interchangeably.

"We should take care not to make the intellect our god; it has of course powerful muscles, but no personality. It cannot lead, it can only serve."

Leonardo da Vinci

When was the last time that you knowingly did something that you **KNEW** was going to make your life worse? We sometimes have to make decisions that will bring short-term pain, but the basis of every decision we make is the assumption that this thing that we are about to do is going to ultimately make our life better. That is why you went to college, got married, have a job ... and do everything that you do.

It is almost as though each of us builds a fleeting image in our minds of the relative value of the possible outcomes of a decision and then a decision that we think will give us the most positive (or least painful) outcome.

"Convictions are more dangerous enemies of truth than lies."

Nietzsche

Because we are more aware of the verbal rational part of our brains, we assume that every part of our minds should be open to the pressure of argument and debate. Because we perceive we are more able to "rely" on reason and logic, we misread the nature and significance of a great deal of our lives. Our inability to control our emotions generally leads us to pretend they aren't there, and unless we can describe a feeling accurately, we dismiss it as "irrational" and therefore not devoutly to be wished.

"Never confuse wisdom with luck."

Ferengi Rule of Acquisition #44

choosing and losing

the big difference

momentum

All this is fine and dandy, and marvellously logical. It all makes sense. That is, until you throw in the curve ball that is known as emotion. Whenever an emotional dynamic rears its ugly head, the whole reasoning process gets put into jeopardy. That is neither bad nor good; just real.

Feel the force

If you believe the world is a hostile place, you don't believe you have a choice and end up protecting yourself against the hostile world.

Where there is a driving force for change, there usually exists a complementary force against it. Gestalt theorists describe this behaviour as resistance. It is not an absence of energy, but an energy that flows in a different direction. When resistance is consciously chosen, it is powerful and constructive. (Contrary to Borg belief, resistance is not futile.)

A great deal of learning comes from recognizing the polarities in resistance. It is necessary for self-regulation, and without it people cannot maintain their boundaries. So when you choose a particular course of action, not only will you need to accept a loss, you will also need to work with the resistance.

So does this suggest that in order to understand what is important to us, we have to experience it first? Maybe we won't know how important it is to us until we don't have it. Many people talk about how important their family become when one of them becomes ill. Or they only allow themselves to think of all the things they have ever wanted to do because they are sick, or come into a great deal of money. There is a reality here, clearly about what we need to survive in the world, and what we have to give up in order to do so. However, how much of that is what we want to have, rather than what we think we should or ought to have?

"Through purely logical thinking we can attain no knowledge whatsoever of the empirical world."

Albert Einstein

choosing and losing

the big difference

momentum

Could we have made a better decision anyway? Who knows? In the real world it is impossible to decide what makes a better decision, because you can see the effects of only one decision unfold in practice. What another decision would have achieved will forever remain unknown.

There is a difference between being a free child and making choices.

Don't mistake the Sixties' "anything goes" attitudes for making choices. Part of the problem for both those living in the Sixties and their children was a plethora of potential choices. I am not sure anyone chose; it seems as though people said, let's try everything, and that potentially is as big a cop-out as following one strict way of being. It's certainly not a choice.

There is also the illusion of choice – 200 channels with nothing on you want to see. If you have been brought up on thin gruel, it's hard for you to step up to a groaning smorgasbord table. Do I deserve to eat this stuff? What and how much can I eat? Eeyore would have probably said that decision making was a mournfully oppressive business.

So does the choice/decision dilemma extend to all parts of our lives? Choosing relationships, for example...

Now here's a big one.

It is only in a close relationship, an intimate one, that we really get the opportunity to see how we act.

Big risk. Potentially big gain. Worth it?

Do we choose people who will accept our controlled story? Do we choose people who will accept and value us? Do we choose people who will let us be ourselves (whoever that might be)? Does the higher the risk mean the more opportunity for growth?

Do we choose anyone, or are we drawn to people without making conscious choices? Sometimes we are drawn to people who will force us into a risk zone. One of the attractions of passion and romance is that they have the potential to take us further, with a higher excitement level, than a companion might. It may even explain some of our attraction to people who are "dangerous".

These decisions are both intuitive and conscious; head and heart.

There are no single victims in long-term relationships; if you examine what may look like a victim, you generally find collusion; like finds like. Both parties are keeping something going; for example, he may be sleeping around, but she is turning a blind eye.

Choosing relationships opens some possibilities and closes others. The question is whether you are choosing the possibilities.

Sometime one masquerades as the other.

Martin felt able to manage anything. He got this feeling by making everything that happened to him of the same magnitude; whether it was missing a train, his coffee being cold, or having a car accident. He saw all these incidents as situations that had to be "got through". In doing this, he felt that nothing could faze him, because it was all the same. This looks like supreme confidence, whereas the truth was that he was so terrified of doing something wrong, or displeasing someone and them rejecting him, that he developed strong controls over his environment so that he would feel nothing. This isn't confidence or self-belief in its truest sense.

Getting your head round things

So what sort of behaviours help you in the choice process?

Stage one has to be getting clear what is going on in your head: what you are experiencing and perceiving. Thinking about things will either help you clarify and maybe even resolve what is going on in your head and/or heart; or it will do the opposite and make you more anxious, and stressed. Even a positive interpretation may only have a short shelf life.

It is very easy to confuse interpretations with data. Action Design describe this as a Ladder of Inference. We tacitly register some data and ignore other data. We impose our own interpretations on the data and draw conclusions from the interpretations. We lose sight of how we came to these conclusions because we do not think about our thinking. Our conclusions lead us to act in ways that produce results that reinforce our assumptions.

We watch, take in information, summarize and select data in our heads, and throw in a few assumptions and reach a conclusion. Quite often we use this spurious data as a basis for further conclusions. So it is possible we could be interpreting based on assumption, not fact. Ability to question and revise is crucial to a constructive interpretation. The better you get at questioning yourself, the easier it becomes to imagine different interpretations, and ones which may be more appropriate to the time you are in now as opposed to when you first experienced the feelings.

Interpretation doesn't allow you to change events; nothing does. However, it does give you the freedom to choose how much importance you attach to which events. You have a number of pieces of information and how you put them together can change the picture and story dramatically.

If we thought about each inference we made, life would pass us by. Our intuitive reasoning is invaluable. But people can and do reach different conclusions, even when they are working from the same pool of data. If you view your conclusions as obvious, no one sees a need to describe how they got there. (With highly intuitive people, they rarely know, unless questioned closely.)

If you become more aware of where your reasoning comes from, you become more aware of how important it is to your thinking in the future. It allows you to see what impacts on you and what you may have missed....

At all times of transition there are points at which two people look at the same thing at the same time, but with entirely different views of its value...

"The keys to the future lie hidden in plain sight because we are blinded by the glare of the present, by what paleontologists call 'the tyranny of the near past' and by other factors that contribute to the distorting lens of attitudes and biases that mediate our perceptions of the world."

Don Michael

How can you talk about the future if you are unwilling to understand the past? Being flexible with the information comes from appreciating that no single event or person is totally responsible for your feelings. Neither is one cause at the root of anything.

In that spirit, try looking at what you have considered important episodes in your life. Ask yourself what made or makes them important. Examine the choices or decisions you made and what was behind them. This is about interpreting your data.

So what makes a helpful interpretation?

◆ Something that has identified both the vulnerable and strong sides of you in the situation.

◆ Something that links aspects of the situation with aspects of your character.

◆ Something that has taken into consideration your underlying filters, and has compensated for them. One that has exposed your true feelings rather than your strategies for hiding your feelings.

This is the hardest one to get to, as over time our defensive patterns can become so ingrained that we believe them to be us. Sometimes this show has had such a long run that we can't remember what we were defending against.

Taking your emotional clothes off is a crucial part in the choice process, and that doesn't happen until you

acknowledge the "unacceptable" emotions that you have been protecting yourself from.

No choice until you have faced these perceived demons.

Feeling free to even consider choice is dependent on the level of power and control we feel we have on ourselves. It is the "I am not worthy" stuff, but don't dismiss the blindingly obvious just because it is blindingly obvious. We often look for dramatic and complex meaning when there is none. Sometimes indeed there is more, but don't dismiss common or garden variety because it seems too simple an answer. It is about going behind the cliché to ask where it comes from and how it affects **YOU**.

The way we feel and how we behave may pivot on the power we attribute to one another.

We feel so tempted, particularly in times of trouble, to trust and depend on people who seem more powerful than we are. However powerful they seem, they are still human, they still have bodily functions, and are subject to the same feelings of overwhelmingness that we are. Missing an opportunity to be in charge of ourselves enhances their power and diminishes ours further.

Corruption begins not in power but in ignorance about that power.

It is as if we carry around in our right hand and left hand pockets two conflicting messages – one says I can do whatever I want, and the other says I am worthless and will submit.

We never seem to know which pocket our hand will dive into. Still it's a step up to agree that you have two options.... When we make a choice, we choose the pocket....

choosing and losing

the big difference

moment um

Unthinkable activities

Failure may be experienced as no more than not achieving what we might. People who feel worthless often experience each failed attempt as if it implies that they themselves are total failures. None of us is sufficiently wise, competent or consistent to escape ever making a mistake, failing or acting stupid. We all have to occasionally endure the embarrassment of helplessness. Getting through these first requires acknowledging what you are doing, and not feeling shame about it.

People these days will encourage you to make more mistakes, but often don't mean it. You are likely to still feel embarrassed, but if feeling stupid is the price you have to pay to try out unorthodox ideas, maybe the helplessness is worthwhile. Thinking the unthinkable, saying the unspeakable and doing the unacceptable are activities that take time and courage. You will undoubtedly make more mistakes and fail more often, but you are also likely to be right and succeed more often.

"A petty fool is nothing but a worldling, but a great fool is a Buddha."

Buddhist saying

"If I am not for myself, who will be for me?
And if I am for myself only, what am I?"

Jewish saying

Thinking the unthinkable; making mistakes; paradoxically these are the things that *increase* not decrease personal power.

Power is the ability to influence and influence is the manifestation of power. Under pressure there are times when we discover that our belief in ourselves is more fragile than we wish. By the same token some situations can surprise us and allow us to see how much influence we really have.

Dominance and submission are not necessarily determined by one person being stronger than the other. It's all in the perception. In situations where people have equal power, the one who lets the other get away with defining the relationship is likely to end up feeling oppressed.

High status/low status.....the raised eyebrow, superior tone of voice etc....suggests that you would have to be mad or stupid to disagree with them. If you accept this threat, of course you will feel dominated. If you want more control over yourself, you get it only by stopping the desire to control or be approved of by others.

If you do this, you are far less likely to experience this feeling of helplessness. When we try to control others, we are most at risk of being exploited by them. We often – both professionally and personally – try to turn the other person into what we want them to be.

Sheldon Kopp suggests sometimes trying to indulge your need for omnipotence, and try telling the person that what you really want is to have everything your own way all of the time. Interesting exercise....

To learn to use power well, or to profit from it when it is ours, we need to stop trying to control others, and

enjoy the freedom power can give when you take charge of yourself.

We do not have to remain subordinate because someone appears to have the upper hand. Power is useless unless it is appropriate to the situation in which we find ourselves. When we try so hard to control things, we are no longer in charge of our lives. However helpless we might be to control events that come to pass, we still have the power to pay attention to the things that matter most to us.

choosing and losing

the big difference

momentum

Contending with powerlessness can exaggerate people's characters by pushing their personal style to extremes. For example, some become so humbled by their helplessness that they become constantly passive and unassuming. Others are so filled with anger at their impotence that they live their lives in a state of chronic irritability.

Most of us are likely to be a little bit of this and a bit of that. While we may try to simplify our characters, we abound in contradictions. The man who never has an unkind word to say who suddenly loses his temper and beats his wife; the church treasurer who turns out to be swindling funds; those who seem to be brutally uncaring risking their lives to rescue a stranger.

Many folk work all the hours they can in the belief that money and success are their only hope of getting the power to allow them to do whatever they want. They often play as hard as they work by getting involved in extreme sports, drugs, or many complex relationships.

Work does not need to be so hard, nor play so risky.

Free living has nothing to do with fighting or complying with authority.

It is about spending as much of your time doing those things that you find personally meaningful, whether that is on your own or with people who matter to you.

"The inner power has far less to do with pleasing the powerful or impressing the powerless than it does with doing as I please. It depends more on experiencing my input than on displaying my output."

Sheldon Kopp

Doing what you would rather be doing will involve you acknowledging your helplessness.

This means making mistakes, extending efforts that do not always pay off, and maybe sometimes experiencing trial and error over inspired intuitive insights. For example, it is hard to distinguish at first go whether someone or something is going to be a major player in our story. In fact sometimes we are really sure that they are and they turn out to be a bit player.

No use getting angry, that's just the way it is.....There is no way you can know everything at first go; you may know something, but it can't be the whole story. What you can't know until it happens is the impact it has.

Phil wrote his Ph.D thesis on authenticity. The challenge of turning on students inspires him periodically, but he doesn't like to feel out of balance with who he now believes he is; such as having to confront a system that doesn't appreciate or value who he is. He feels frustrated by the hoops he has to go through to be successful in the system which have nothing to do with the students. He is well liked, but has huge problems dealing with the politics of the situation.

He has made a choice about what is important to him. He now has a choice about what he does with that.

Here is a selection of items from Sheldon Kopp's Laundry List. It's the sort of thing that gets sent to you in an e-mail, alleged to have come from the Dalai Lama. No such claims are made for these comments. They are simply a summary of attitudes that are helpful in becoming more conscious of the things that matter to you.

◆ Everyone has dreams of triumph and humiliation.

◆ Be confident that you will continue to make mistakes.

◆ You need to take responsibility for both your power and your helplessness.

◆ There is no way for anyone to be totally on top of every aspect of their lives.

◆ No one is ever totally safe from harm.

◆ If you learn to tell false alarms from real ones, you can decide which risks are worth taking.

◆ Everyone is helpless when it comes to predicting what will happen next.

◆ No one feels safe being completely open.

◆ We frequently form negative attachments rather than face the fear of being alone.

choosing and losing

the big difference

momentum

- Inner power has less to do with pleasing others than it does with doing as we please.

- Defying or complying with authority has nothing to do with living freely.

- A person can't do what can't be done.

- There is no way of getting all you want.

- You can't have anything unless you let go of it.

- You only get to keep what you give away.

- You don't really control anything.

- You are free to do what you like. You need only face the consequences.

- Making a choice is about choosing the things that suit your beliefs and principles, regardless of their popularity or unpopularity.

- The more you accept yourself, the more likely you are to lose the "superior" perfectionism that often makes you feel inadequate.

- As you stop competitively comparing yourself to others, you lose interest in judging what or who is right or wrong.

- Whether you make a choice or a decision is not the fundamental point.

- What matters is that you know what process you have been through, and the implications for where you have ended up.

- Doing what you would rather be doing will probably involve both choice and decision.

- In coming to a realization about what is really important to you, it looks like it is inescapable that you will at some point have to choose and lose. Choosing means a new state, and therefore something will be left behind.

- New skin does not flourish until the old has been sloughed off.

"AND STILL, AMONG IT ALL, SNATCHES OF LOVELY
OBLIVION, AND SNATCHES OF RENEWAL

ODD, WINTRY FLOWERS UPON THE WITHERED STEM,
YET NEW STRANGE FLOWERS

SUCH AS MY LIFE HAS NOT BROUGHT FORTH
BEFORE, NEW BLOSSOMS OF ME."

D.H. Lawrence

the story so far …

"WHO ARE YOU?" SAID THE CATERPILLAR.
THIS WAS NOT AN ENCOURAGING OPENING FOR A
CONVERSATION. ALICE REPLIED, RATHER SHYLY,
"I-I HARDLY KNOW, SIR, JUST AT PRESENT – AT LEAST I
KNOW WHO I WAS WHEN I GOT UP THIS MORNING
BUT I THINK I MUST HAVE BEEN CHANGED SEVERAL
TIMES SINCE THEN."
"WHAT DO YOU MEAN BY THAT?" SAID THE
CATERPILLAR, STERNLY. "EXPLAIN YOURSELF!"
"I CAN'T EXPLAIN MYSELF, I'M AFRAID, SIR," SAID ALICE,
"BECAUSE I'M NOT MYSELF, YOU SEE."

Lewis Carroll, *Alice in Wonderland*

the story so far ...

Ever felt like Alice? It is so hard to describe or explain yourself when you don't know who you are....

Inside we often struggle with the effort of the pull between living a life doing what we should be doing and doing what we would rather be doing.

What creates this struggle? What does lie beneath?

Finding and making the Big Difference means knowing where you are and what are your primary components. Without knowing that, you are choosing to be different from what?

This chapter is about understanding your story.

Telling the story you'd rather be telling

"Each of us is branded by particular experience that we need to somehow complete."

Michael Rabiger

Human beings across the world have several things in common:

- We are born.
- We laugh.
- We cry.
- We seek acknowledgment.
- We die.

The elements are the same; the way they get played out is what creates an individual tale.

"You may ask yourself, well how did I get here?
You may tell yourself, this is not my beautiful house
You may tell yourself, this is not my beautiful wife…"

Talking Heads

Telling the story of your life so far. How has it been for you? The earth probably hasn't moved enough, otherwise you wouldn't be searching for something else. What does it take to tell your story? Like any film, it needs and has:

- plot
- pace

- characters

- incidents.

It probably has a beginning, but whether you want to end the current story and start a new one, or make the current one take a new turn, is part of your search.

"The first thing
The last thing.
Start from where you are."

Dale Pendell

The plot of a story generally reveals the character: in our lives, the situations we find ourselves in reveal our patterns of behaviour. Your story is told through your actions and reactions, intuitions and feelings. Recognizing the plot and patterns of behaviour is essential in making choices about what you want. You need to know where you are before you can move on.

It also helps if you have a structure which you feel you can dismantle yourself and replace with another, should that be necessary. First you need to recognize the structure, what holds it together, and what would help you dismantle it.

When you examine the way that you have responded to various situations in your life, you find that often the same theme underlies the way you have behaved in all of them.

Understanding this context for our behaviour is a huge help in understanding what has motivated us in various situations and what the impact of that has been and might be in the future. If it is something we can change and are willing to, can we also accept it if we can't change…?

Inner conflict and unhappiness are normal and necessary parts of the human experience and are usually the very dissatisfaction that forms the basis for a search for something different. So without getting in touch with the more difficult parts of our story, it's unlikely we will ever know what we don't want, let alone what we do want.

Avoidance is not the same as accepting something that is hard for us. Provocative events can leave us with emotional responses a long time after the event. Knowing the events and their impact helps us calibrate their future impact.

Our emotional architecture should not be seen as a nuisance.

It is the key to our lives. We are made up of unseen forces and silent messages that shape us.

Awareness comes from the struggle to describe what is, not what should be.

We tell and hear stories of our lives every day. We are characters in some, directors in others and cinemagoers for many. Sometimes the roles get a little confused and we lose our place in the script.

Living the life you choose is about identifying the plotline and the character you are. It is about being ready to improvise with whatever the accidents of the bigger lifescript throw in, and weave them into your own; not to allow them to blow your script apart. How might they develop both you and other characters? How might they advance the plot?

"I've lived too long, and acted and felt, to say this one is right and that one wrong. I've had enough of living according to the image others show me of myself. I've resolved on autonomy, I demand independence in interdependence."

Albert Camus

Most of our deeply held beliefs and stories come from childhood. Integrating this directness and vulnerability with the understanding, wisdom and tolerance of an adult is a powerful goal, but damn hard to do. Some people never get to the understanding and wisdom bit, some are so stuck with the impact of a child's story that it's hard for them to shift.

Many of us never get past the child perspective. This is a perspective that is very self-centred; focused on "me" and "being done to". There is also an element of excitement and spontaneity, but most people who are stuck there seem to lose this.

The child has no sense that anyone else's perspective is important; they have no empathy for others, apart from understanding what is necessary to get their own way. They have no sense of compromise. They have no concept of "later"; everything has to be done now. Their needs have to be met **NOW**, however that needs to happen.

(Ever felt that desperate need to have a problem resolved or a want met **NOW**, no matter how irrational your desperation might seem?)

Others appear powerful, without fears or weaknesses. The positive aspects of this way of seeing the world are senses of pleasure, the moment, vulnerability, and innocence. Consequently, when operating from this view of the world, you see others as more powerful and less vulnerable than yourself. This leads to a strategy of defence and protection, often from a "victim" point of view.

It is unlikely that we would ever lose the child's perspective, nor would we want to. The adult perspective, doing what you want to without fear and with confidence, is largely about knowing what perspective is appropriate for the situation you find yourself in. Adults get a sense of satisfaction from seeing that there is more than one way to view a situation. An adult perspective is marked by applied experience, practicality, self-knowledge and an empathy with others' fears and vulnerabilities. In extremis, it can be rigid, controlling and judgemental.

"Achieving is about what you do; deserving is about what you are."

Hilary Austen

Who knows who deserves and who doesn't? To try to answer what you think you deserve is probably as useless as trying to decide whether or not you are right or wrong, or good or bad.

If good or bad exist, than we are both.

We love to judge and hate to be judged.

The worst case scenario is an extreme child scenario (victim) combined with an extreme adult (controlling and judgemental). It is easy to want to be a successful businessperson and want to set sail on a square-rigger for the Virgin Islands at the same time.

Think about moments in your life when you have adopted either of these standpoints. See if you perceive a pattern. Are there certain events or people that trigger those particular responses? Can you see a reasoning behind the pattern?

In narrator mode

One way to work out where you are standing is to take on the role of the narrator. The narrator's role in theater, stories or film is to describe what is happening in the story in a way that presents an objective view that stops the audience taking sides. It's the part of us that says part of me wants to never see that woman again, and part of me wants to marry her tomorrow. Becoming a narrator in your life is being able to see all the conflicting and competing emotions you are facing, being able to understand and see them for what they are. It is your reality check. Bearing in mind, of course, that there rarely is an absolute reality or "truth".

Mandy Aftel describes this as "the sum of competing differences, which have certain irreducible elements in common".

Too much or too little self-observation is likely to take you either into victim mode or control mode. Neither of these helps you see the story...Yes, it's a question of balance; once again, in understanding ourselves, one of the hardest concepts to stick with is the lack of absolutes, and the continuous need for balance. It doesn't mean losing extremes, it means knowing when you are standing at an extreme, and what the implications for standing there are. Being a narrator for yourself is not about missing out or excluding the emotional experience; quite the reverse, it is about including it in that context. This demands the emotion of the child and the understanding of the adult.

Of course we are all perfectly capable of distorting our stories. As soon as we have gone into a blame or externalization mode, we have lost the opportunity to tell the reality. To do that we have to include the personal accountability for things that we have done or felt. An accurate narrator is aware of and asks themselves questions (that they try to answer) about their role in the situation – what did I do to contribute to this? It is not about a passive storyteller, it is about remaining active.

Are we creating and bending our perceptions of people to fit our story?

"Do you understand what you say?
Yes if I listen attentively."

An Ideal Husband

When people don't do what we want them to do, we have to lose the false story we have created for them before we can deal with a new one. The same is true of ourselves: if we have created a persona for ourselves and we realize that it is not who we want to be, we first have to deal with the loss of the fantasy person before we can move to our new reality.

Yesterday may be over but the memories remain.

Dealing with the loss is not about forgetting, it is about preserving the memory for what it was, when it was; not imbuing it with the power to stay the same in any similar or different situation.

It was what it was.

There is no final decision on anyone, self or others.

Tell the documentary, not the docudrama.

"You should say what you mean," the March Hare went on.
"I do," Alice hastily replied, "at least, I mean what I say – that's the same thing you know."
"Not the same thing a bit!" said the Hatter.

Alice in Wonderland

The way we tell our stories is fundamental to understanding what is really happening to us. The words we use, the pictures we conjure up, the narrative patterns that we weave are big clues.

> "Those who do not have power over the story that dominates their lives, power to retell it, rethink it, deconstruct it, joke about it, and change it as times change, truly are powerless, because they cannot think new thoughts."
>
> Salman Rushdie

The way we describe our lives is inextricably linked to the way we live them. If you listen to the way others tell their stories you can hear many pointers about the things that are important to them. Recognizing themes in others helps you to recognize themes in yourself. Looking out really helps you to look in.

The key is in the action or behaviour, not the words.

Character is revealed in deed and action, not talk.

Debbie walked confidently into the room. In a split second she had surveyed the terrain and decided which item of furniture would show her off to best advantage. She sat down and flashed a smile of greeting.

The first mention of her mother caused a brief frown, quickly followed by a statement that that was all under control now and that things were proceeding as one might expect. Her conversation was peppered with phrases that said very little, in an extremely rational and logical way, but which effectively shut down any further questioning unless you were really ready to probe.

Expressions of warmth, whether physical or verbal, were totally discouraged. In fact, warmth seemed to be absent from her persona.

Debbie was in fact trying to deal with the complex range of emotions she was experiencing as she was arranging for her mother, who had Alzheimer's disease, to go into special care. A highly competent and effective manager, this episode had surfaced many issues for Debbie about being taken care of, about reality and fantasy. One of the biggest issues for her was her conflict between having the ability to cope and organize pretty much anything and anybody, and being recognized and valued as this person; and her desire to occasionally have someone do it for her.

the story so far . . .

the big difference

momentum

Dealing with this maelstrom of irrationality made her so uncomfortable that she sought even more control by shutting down any invitations to talk about herself. She did not really feel as though she could trust her feelings not to emerge, they felt so close to the surface.

Her desire to control this side of her led her into behaving in a similar way with her colleagues and team at work.

She was coping, but at a huge cost to both herself and her colleagues. For Debbie to be able to move on, she needed to examine her story. She needed to look at and connect with the strong emotions that were lurking so close to the surface, and work out which of them belonged to her past and which were appropriate to her now.

When she finally did this, she actually felt more in control by having let go and understood her feelings than when she was trying to hold them back.

Well, I would say that, wouldn't I...It is true. It isn't meant to sound glib and painless. It certainly wasn't for Debbie. However it was important for her to see her story as it was then, and as it is now. That was the key for her.

Exhale here before you take in any more....

It's a wonderful emotion

Actions never spring out of nowhere. When they seem unexpected, they usually come from a subplot about which you were unaware.

"A chance word or a sigh are just as much evidence as a speech or a murder: the life they reveal ceases to be secret and enters the realm of action."

E.M. Forster

What evokes memories? Maybe a better question is, what evokes the emotions that come with the memories?

What is it about the films *It's a Wonderful Life* or *Billy Elliot* that makes so many people cry?

How we deal with information that others present is always important to the story. If someone presents you with characteristics that you don't like and yet you are still drawn to them, are you suffering from the delusion that you will be the one to change them?

Real engagement with a person is not possible unless you believe their story and are able to hear it from their point of view. It is a lot easier to absorb it into your frame than leaving their story as their own.

Writers are always told to write about things they are familiar with, as we are much more vivid about describing our own experiences. They are 'real' to us. Many writers are incapable of doing anything else. Telling their story is a way of expressing themselves and sometimes validating in an external way what has happened to them. Hanif Kureishi has written several scripts and books which all seem to unashamedly reflect his life experience in some way. Does it make him more able to feel comfortable with himself? Who knows?

Stories are linked plots. The plots are incidents or events and the story is what links them. We are sometimes good at describing one or the other; for example, good at describing the events that have happened to us, with no context; no description of thoughts, feelings, impact. Or good at describing all the attending thoughts and feelings, again without context.

Even our normal ways of thinking and expressing ourselves are woefully inadequate for describing our present or past circumstances, let alone finding a way to describe a possible future. The filters and frames we develop are a type of shorthand to let us manage and know what to expect in the world. If experience and expectation colour these lenses, how can we change the lens to see things differently? We all use our data filters to take in and view information as "true". So in every discussion,

each individual has their own take on the "truth".

"History is what you remember, and if you don't think it is being revised all the time, you haven't paid enough attention to your own memory. When you remember something, you don't remember the thing itself – you just remember the last time you remembered it."

John Barlow

the story so far . . .

the big difference

momentum

THINGS EXIST ONLY BY VIRTUE OF

THE SPACE AROUND THEM ...

One artist, Aviva Sklan, explained that when she was learning to draw and wasn't quite sure how to commit an object to paper, she would look at the space around it, and that would enable her to see the object for how it filled that space.

Looking at the script outline often helps us understand the plot line, rather than getting lost in character details....

"The problems are solved, not by giving new information but by arranging what we have known since long."

Wittgenstein

A plot point is a moment where the story veers off unexpectedly in another direction. They are powerful because they divert a story that appears predictable.

Our reactions to a plot point in our lives vary from excitement to panic and fear. Our fear of the unknown usually creates the fear.

The inner eye is the frequently silent cinema in your head. It replays the material of memory in a starkly truthful way. Though it may not be a factually accurate record of the original events, this is immaterial, because it represents powerfully the way you now perceive them.

A character is said to develop when they learn enough from their experiences to make a significant change of behaviour and action in situations. When we become short sighted or lost for ideas, it is often because present issues in our lives seem unyielding.

Even glaciers move...

"Artistic identity is the source of creativity that each person carries within. Shaped by temperament and biographical circumstances, it sends one on a quest for answers to the unfinished business in one's life."

Michael Rabiger

Not losing the plot

Keeping journals is a popular way of logging what occurs to you.
That may well be all it is. A log; no more, no less. If we have been
honest with our feelings and thoughts, and look at our writing over a
period of time, we may see a pattern of thoughts which allows us to
interpret or think further. Two big ifs there: honest writing, and a
desire to make something of the writing, rather than it being the end
in itself.

When we describe them to someone else, we occasionally put a
different filter on to describe them, depending on how we want the
other person to hear us. We do this knowingly sometimes, other
times not. Sometimes we think we are disguising ourselves,
sometimes the veneer is easy to see through. How much of that is
conscious or subconscious is very situational. Who knows? Well, you
would if you had the opportunity to see and hear you.
Understanding yourself well enough to know what makes you is the
only way you can choose. Otherwise how would you know what it
was you wanted?

However, the things you hear or perceive are pointers for you, not
necessarily data about the individuals. We hear things in our own
framework, so when someone describes their life as a Bogart movie, I
will see my favourite Bogart movies, and interpret them through my
eyes. My mental models are what guide my thoughts.

"For now we see through a glass darkly; but then face to face:
now I know in part;
but then I shall know even as also I am known."

Paul the Apostle

Time spent on you increases your awareness of how you are, rather than how you think you should be. Some writers have all the plots figured out before they start to write. Quite often, characters take on a life of their own and begin living out something that was not in the original plot. Planning and preparing, or living out an old plotline, or someone else's story, stops us from engaging in our true story. Focusing on who we are and what is happening to us allows for new twists and more excitement in the story.

We tell stories to make our place in life. Sometimes a plot line intervenes that we perceive to be harmful to us. One of the options we have when faced with this is to kill the storyline.

Things we do to kill our stories, that is, stop anything we perceive untoward from happening (sometimes known as defence mechanisms):

- Blocking
- Blame someone or something external
- Denying
- Make a joke out of "it"
- Hedging
- Attack
- Changing the subject
- Lie
- Lower the stakes/wimping
- Gossip
- Join in
- Justify

These actions have a couple of things in common:

- they are all about avoiding acceptance of a perceived difficult situation;
- they leave you with the misguided perception that doing them will keep you in control.

If you can see that you have built these mechanisms to avoid a particular storyline, such as making a commitment or dealing with conflict, then

you can at least choose whether you continue the act or not.

Trouble is, once you know that you are wasting your time, it becomes harder to defend your actions. (Of course, that's why we tend to not want to be aware of our defence mechanisms, because then the awareness makes them look irrational and we might have to face the very thing we were defending ourselves against. Much easier to pretend…but then, you can't choose, and you are unlikely to be doing what you'd rather be doing…..unless you have chosen to make a lifetime career out of never facing up to anything. Actually, that is a common career choice. If it is yours, then I'm not sure why you are reading this.)

"right that's enough it's far too late to be here and I'm knackered...simplicity and sanity are not necessarily consummations devoutly to be wished – good job – I'm complicated and barking mad for sure. hurrah."

BigRazBird

So how can we get a better perspective on how we are telling the story?

If we stay with the cinema metaphor, when directors want to see how a film is going, they look at their dailies – film that has been shot that day.

Looking at a day or even a period in your life, take one shot from your "dailies" and make sense of it.

What would constitute a key frame for you?

Why would you say "I like this frame better than another"?

This understanding of how we view our stories helps clarify what things attract and repel – and both of these are important in determining our personal story. We tend to focus on the positive frames as the places to look for things that are important to us. The need to acknowledge the things we dislike about ourselves as well as things we are proud of is part of strengthening ourselves and being realistic about who we are.

What are the bad bits that we want to edit?

What makes us keep the "good" bits in?

If I want to change the way I see something, I need to change my frame of reference. Changing our behaviour or actions only changes things briefly and doesn't create sustainable change. In order for us to really know who we are and what is important to us, we need to understand where we come from, what has shaped our thoughts and feelings, and the impact that has on the way in which we see the world.

This isn't about navel gazing, it is about thinking beyond what is immediately visible; what is below the tip of the iceberg. It was what lay underneath the water that destroyed the *Titanic*, not what was visible above the water.

What events brought you to this place and position?

Has something been lost?

Has something been improved?

What has been difficult or uncomfortable?

When we think about what really matters to us, we could make a list of the way we frame things, such as:

◆ I cannot trust anyone.

◆ I am not worthy.

◆ I have to do everything perfectly.

◆ I cannot put myself first.

◆ I must keep everyone happy.

◆ Whatever happens, I can deal with it.

Most of these tend to be negative. They come from many places, e.g. parents, teachers, friends, media. It takes only one message from a perceived authority at an impressionable age to render something as law in our heads. For example, one woman asked me if a strong message from her childhood that little girls should be seen and not heard might affect the fact that she found it hard to speak up at work meetings…

We can take any message like this and make it a truth for us, and until we question it, it will remain so. This can become a mental model that controls the way we see things and consequently the way we respond to them.

Once an assumption is in place, it colours everything you do, and the way you see others. Moving from one position to another ain't easy.

Just a word of caution here: whatever messages you have received, you will have sent out as many. It is worth considering how the messages you have sent will have impacted on others, and maybe kept a destructive flow of events in place. It usually takes two parties to produce a problem.

Think about others. They define us more than we realize. What you value and dislike in others can say more about who you are than trying to describe yourself. What is our intent when we describe ourselves?

To convince?

To persuade?

To seduce?

"Everyday I write the book."

Elvis Costello

The cutting room floor

We do like to edit our lives, in order to feel comfortable with the script. Sometimes when we edit, we take out what we perceive to be "bad bits". We don't always enhance the "good bits". We usually don't know how we would classify "bad" or "good", but we still edit. Who is watching the film that we edit? What is bad at one moment may be good in another. Is it a smart move to leave everything in the film? Well, that might prove difficult, as we cannot hold every single thought in active memory. The question is, how do we sort the inputs we get?

Are you editing out something that is central to you or something that *was* central to you at the time you registered it? Is it something that will matter going forward? It does not mean it matters more or less on its own merits, it is whether its importance at the time of recording is the same as its importance now or in the future.

Sometimes an edit is crucial to get a fix on a new reality.

An edit may not be a cut, it may be a joining of two pieces to make a new picture or scene, as opposed to what seems to be a violent deletion. Putting two pieces together can sometimes give you a completely new view, or a different perspective on an old one.

(Interestingly, in the film world, the Americans refer to film editing as "cutting" which puts the emphasis on separation. In Australia and Britain, film is "joined", with the emphasis on bringing together.)

The discernment about where and what to cut or keep is all. It would seem that sudden disruption of reality can be useful in helping us to adapt to change, so when you do have to make a cut, what is that makes it an appropriate one? What things would it be useful for us to look at when discerning what we keep in our story?

Let us suppose four key editing criteria (adapted from Walter Murch):

◆ **Emotion:** it is true to the emotion of the moment. If the story is about you, it is about you in that moment and therefore should reflect that.

◆ **Forward movement:** it advances your story in some way.

◆ **Rhythm:** it reflects an appropriate sense of what is rhythmically right for that time, and for you at that time.

◆ **Relativity:** it takes into account the relationships between and the dynamics of the situation and the people involved.

Each criterion has an importance of its own.

The interconnection between the criteria is strong, and stronger between the first two than the second two. Emotion has to be the thing you preserve at all costs. It is what makes the scene yours, and if you have to sacrifice any of the other criteria for the sake of this one, so be it.

It is you.

If the emotional side is right, then often the rhythm and relativity go hand in hand. Don't give up emotion for forward movement in your story. Don't give up your story for appropriate rhythm, and don't give up rhythm for relativity.

If you are telling your story for yourself, the presentation takes on a different skew than if you are telling your story to an audience. Maybe this is situational, and there are times when you will choose to tell your story to an audience. The difference is whether you do this knowingly, in full cognition and acceptance of the consequences, or whether you do it unknowingly.

the big difference

momentum

We are great at doing the Houdini thing, where we create such a good show that neither we nor others look at what is really happening. He didn't want people to look at where he was actually undoing his chains so he created something distracting for people to feast their eyes on. "No, don't look there, look here!!" This is what magicians call "misdirection".

We are all capable of high levels of misdirection, to self and others. Why do we not want them or others to see? What is it we don't want them to see?

Understanding what we choose to misdirect helps our awareness. Again, this is not a positive point about ourselves; but knowing means knowing; warts and all.

Beyond the frame

It is easy to get distracted by detail, and for all that it is crucial to experience the moment, you need to know when it is time to step back and get perspective. This does not mean losing the feelings you have had, or the story, rhythm or relativity; it means putting them into a bigger picture so you can see you better. It's the equivalent of sleeping on it, or leaving bread to rise……

It's hard to separate out what you wish to be there from what is actually there, but we need to see how the story actually looks "on screen". Sometimes it takes another person to help with that.

This is almost like a film-test screening, where you test audience reactions, and also see things you haven't seen before.

What would capture for you what Cartier Bresson called "the decisive moment"?

Are you ready to say that I like this scene better than that?

Am I telling what I would rather be telling?

Am I doing what I would rather be doing?

"It is as hard to see one's self as to look backwards without turning around."

Thoreau

You cannot change the past, but you can change the story you have made out of the past.

What completely different assumption could you make about what happened for you in past situations that would change your other assumptions?

You don't begin with meaning, you end with it......

Telling your story involves understanding what has happened for you, the context in which it happened, and its impact on your current way of being. Telling and understanding what your story means to you helps you to decide what story you want to tell in the future and what you will have to do in order to make the story happen.

Living and telling the story you'd rather be telling.

**"IT IS ONLY WITH THE HEART THAT
ONE CAN SEE RIGHTLY.
WHAT IS ESSENTIAL IS
INVISIBLE TO THE EYE."**

Antoine de Saint Exupery

the story so far . . . .

the big difference

momentum

take no notice of the man behind the curtain …

take no notice of the man behind the curtain …

We all suffer the crisis of discovering that life is not all we had been led to believe it would be…at many times; adolescence, mid-life crisis, and just about any time we feel confused or that life has let us down. Nothing makes sense any more. Sometimes we cling to a hope of re-establishing an idealized vision of the world; sometimes we set out to become the person one should be in the quixotic struggle with what is. We set out to get rid of all the ambiguities in ourselves and the world around us so that we can make life meaningful, understandable and manageable. We often try to delay our rude awakening into the world, sometimes for our whole lives.

The way we live in the world means we take things into our bodies and put them out in the world as something else. One person's fantasy is another's reality.

Doing what we would rather be doing sometimes then becomes a fantasy in itself. It is worth looking at some of the behaviours, thoughts and feelings that constitute "fantasies" for us. You also have to be a little crazy to start something brand new. Fantasy fuels the creative, innovative and exciting process necessary to turn ideas into reality.

It means looking at whether the fantasies are things we would really want to do, but don't, for any number of reasons, feel able to achieve; or whether we create fantasies to avoid dealing with difficult issues. Of course, it may not be an either/or situation. The two things could be hopelessly intertwined. No right or wrong. It isn't good or bad to fantasize. Being aware of how what you create impacts on your ability to choose is critical. Having a fantasy about winning the lottery and buying an island in the Caribbean may or may not be within your grasp. The key event in this is out of your hands; that is whether your lottery ticket comes up. This makes it difficult for you to realistically choose it as a life option, unless you are choosing to be fatalistic....

So where does the need for fantasy come from?

Anthony Storr suggests that an inner world of fantasy must be regarded as part of an individual's biological inheritance. When an individual's subjective reality becomes completely divorced from the external reality, we call them mad. On the other hand, if we suppress the inner world too much, we become totally compliant with external reality; we regard the external world as something to which we must adapt, so our individuality disappears and life becomes meaningless.

"Of course it's insane. That's why it's the only thing to do."

Yossarian in *Catch 22*

Sometimes we do look at others and describe their actions as mad... So how mad are we, and what impact does that have?

In terms of making the Big Difference, understanding our fantasies, what they represent, and how they impact on us is fundamental to having the awareness of who we are, how we express that, and how we want to express it.

Knowing whether we are all decoration and no tree, or even finding the tree under the decoration, is a part of knowing who you are.

"Oh body swayed to music
Oh brightening glance
How can we know
The dancer from the dance?"

W.B. Yeats

In the face of repeated experiences that become overwhelming, or that threaten our perceived safety, we come to depend on self-restricting, risk-avoiding, fantasy-bound attitudes and behaviours. (We won't call them this, of course. We call them "ways of coping", plans, or are not cognisant of them.)

Rollo May describes this as "pseudo-innocence".

The pseudo-innocent denies his or her own power, puts their faith in "divine providence", and pretends that this is either the best or worst of all possible worlds. This brings a false sense of order to what feels like a chaotic life situation. These defences prevent any possibility for growth or making any difference, let alone a big one.

Sure, there are times in our lives when we do need coping strategies to get through a situation, but if that coping strategy becomes a way of being that denies the world on a full-time basis, we never move on. Helplessness and nostalgic longing keep us in a childlike position where we insist on someone else taking care of a person who is so "frail".

Whenever these core illusions are threatened, we suffer anxiety and pain. It is almost as though life without illusions would be totally unbearable.

Even on its simplest level – without imagining what we might do if we won the lottery, or how it would feel to spend an evening with the film or rock star of our choice – life seems a little dull. (It was so hard not to name names in that last sentence; some people's fantasies are other people's nightmares. How would an evening with Madonna sound for you?…)

When you reach the stage where you can no longer tell what is real and what isn't, the confusion and bewilderment become very strong. That feeling of vulnerability often leads us to create new fantasies. (Since the old ones may not be real, why not have some real fantasies …You can never have enough windmills in the world.)

Often, accomplished people wake up one morning and ask themselves why they have chosen a way of life that does not suit them. Beneath a veneer of self-confidence lies doubt about whether they are worth anything at all. They often have no clue as to whether they are living a fantasy or not. Their boundaries have disappeared.

At its most extreme form this can become scary as it feels like all the goalposts in your world have shifted.

Joe is a highly successful executive in a transnational corporation. He has recently been promoted, and on the surface looks happy enough. Scratch a little deeper. It is gradually beginning to dawn on him that he is unhappy with the people he works with, and the work he produces.

"I am so tired. I feel as though I am spinning, no, hurtling into a downward spiral. I don't know how to stop it. I just want to curl up in a corner somewhere.

"Where did it start? What the hell is my job? I feel as though I am going to fall over any minute, but if I tell someone, I will fall over. It's getting harder and harder to live with confidence. When they promoted me, I was on top of the world. As soon as I saw the job, I knew it was undoable. My pride was so strong that I thought, of course I can do it."

Just another story from the naked city.

Most of us do have only regular stories. Sometimes we long for the drama. Sometimes we create it to feel special. Sometimes issues that we are struggling with seem so mundane, and yet we still struggle with them. Surely exciting problems would at least make us more interesting? Would people be interested in helping us more? Then they might take the problem away........See the flow?

What do you know about Joe from these extracts?

Actually you know very little as there is very little data in this account. But you will have made a whole lot of inferences from the words he has used, your experience of life, and wherever you are now, that will lead you to various assumptions. Are they questions or issues that you have either experienced or seen in others?

Chances are, you will learn more about yourself from the assumptions you make than you will about Joe.

What connections can you make about the assumptions you have made and the way you experience the world?

take no notice of the man behind the curtain...

the big difference

What fantasies has he created about work and how he should be behaving that have led him to this place? These aren't necessarily big fantasies about being the CEO; they are fantasies about who you are supposed to be; what you are supposed to achieve; whether you are "special" enough.

Special delivery

Special. The more you write special, the weirder the spelling looks. So when we say special, what is it we are describing? For some it is an expression of individuality that gives them identity.

If we have used the illusion of being special to keep us going in the world, to have the "special" taken away leaves us with nothing. We all fool ourselves at times. It is hard to stay aware of yourself when you believe your own fooling.

Special is something that denotes a difference in you from other people. Something that would make them want to be with you more than with someone else. Something that they would want; and also something that you find attractive.

Every person is an individual and different, so the self-help books tell you. Sometimes we create a fantasy difference, or don't know what the real one is. Whatever the motivation, it becomes part of our protection, our inner self (whatever that really is), and in extremis can lead us away from what is really different about us as an individual, because we are looking for something overly dramatic.

We aren't helped in this by media images. They feed our desire to either be a special category and belong there, or be able to do something no one else has done. For example, to bear the "tortured soul of an artist", the "orphan", the "geek", the Yorkshireman, "I'll always be there for you"……

Once you identify someone or something as special, it can rob it of the ability to be itself, multi-faceted and in the moment. Once you call a bird a blue jay, you never see the bird again, you see a blue jay. Naming something gives it a different place. As soon as you name it, you frame it.

take no notice of the man behind the curtain...

the big difference

momentum

Being able to describe your fantasy helps to engage it.

If what you want to do is experience it, you don't need a frame; it just is. Being labelled affects the fantasy, and stops you getting in touch with what you are, "special" or otherwise…

What does it leave you expecting in terms of fantasy about how the world is and what you can expect?

Sometimes it takes the form of a search for a magic way to make people care about us. If only we could be so beautiful, have impressive achievements, do exactly what "they" want, or get "them" to do what we want, then we could live happily ever after.

We look for people who are sufficiently wise and kind to take care of us. Repeated disappointment hurts, but most of the time dealing with that feels better than being on your own. Most people are terrified by the thought of taking care of themselves, and yet espouse the dream that they want to be free. Primary delusion.

Mark had many stories to tell about people who had let him down or tried to thwart him. "Look at my older brother, I was always being compared to him. I never stood a chance. He wasn't much of a support either; too busy revelling in his glory. My ex-wife was only interested in me while I was successful and had the trappings of glory. As for my so-called pal Mike, well he never missed an opportunity to put one over on me at work, although he thought I didn't notice."

Mark took an almost self-righteous pride in proving someone else was responsible for his unhappiness. It seemed as though it was only worth him feeling miserable when he could prove it was someone else's fault. He seemed convinced that making his own decisions would mess up his life.

When confronted with the fact that maybe his dependence on others had already made a mess of his world, he concurred and added: "It's not my fault that the people I trust and turn to for support let me down. How am I supposed to know who to trust?"

Was it not his "fault"? Who chose the players in his life? Was their behaviour real or imagined?

Paying too much attention to what others think and feel may mean we risk knowing what we really want for ourselves.

No human being is pure of thought and action. Whatever we present consciously, the counterpoint exists subconsciously. Part of understanding what is behind the curtain means acknowledging "the dark side".

Fantasies are not only Pollyanna-like, they can also be paranoid. In this delusional world, it is not that everything will be OK, it is that everyone or everything may be harmful to you. This paranoia leads you to confuse being scared with being in danger, and to harm others who are either friendly or indifferent. This often gets played out in feelings of envy and distrust.

The danger with this, or any all-embracing view of the world, is that you lose the opportunity to see how negative events are as much a part of your life as positive ones. Turning them into demons or angels negates their value. It is more to do with understanding what it is about them that leaves you scared, or feeling the need to create a fantasy to protect you.

> Michael believed that the only thing that got him out of control was alcohol. Listening to him talk, you would see that actually being let down by people he trusted was much more likely to get him out of control. What that meant for him was double the talking at double the speed, and a strongly expressed desire to get the hell out of wherever he was. Run. It did seem important to him that he was mellow, as this was the myth he had created for himself to stop other people hurting him; the "I can cope with all of this stuff; nothing fazes me…" Therefore the out-of-control mechanism had to be outside of himself, but one he could administer; that is, alcohol.

In trying to make life more livable, we make other people or things responsible or to blame; conversely we make ourselves more important and special by dramatizing and/or fantasizing around our situation.

"A world that can be explained even with bad reasons is a familiar world."

Albert Camus

Creating castles in the air

Given then that we may harbour romantic notions of ourselves and who we think we ought to be – able to do anything, devil may care, mellow – we need to look at our responses to fantasy and illusion, how we know what we know, and the effect it has.
We tend to respond to this in three basic ways:

◆ **rationally** – by thinking about things using logic and consistency as benchmarks;

◆ **empirically** – by experiencing things through our senses;

◆ **metaphorically** – by using an intuitive grasp of situations in which we are open to symbols and stories with many layers of meaning.

We generally use all three ways, but when faced with new things and uncertainties, and the first two methods do not yield results, we try the third. This is what sometimes takes us into the realms of fantasy. It is a fine line to walk between imagining what something may be like and then believing that that is how it is. The saying goes that neurotics build castles in the air, and psychotics walk in.

Culturally, metaphor is often the only way people express difficult thoughts such as a love for their country, or a belief in a deity. For example, Americans can go to jail for desecrating their flag because the flag is a symbol of their country; some people partake of wafer and wine as the body and blood of Christ.

So sometimes the metaphor is a way of expressing imagination in the only way it feels possible at that time.

Imagination is crucial in terms of thinking the unthinkable, and what might be. Grounding and expressing that in reality is the harder part.

"All metaphor breaks down somewhere. That is the beauty of it. It is touch and go with the metaphor, and until you've lived with it long enough, you don't know when it is going."

Robert Frost

It might be helpful to consider the kind of metaphors you use or are attracted to. It is also helpful to see where they can't be applied. So for example, do you see life as "a lucky dip", or a "game of chance"? This might lead you to believe that choice was not in your power but was dependent on the "spin of the wheel".

Telling your story and understanding what is real and fantasy is essential for being in a position to choose. Knowing what you want as a reality or a fantasy?

Think about a metaphor in your life and ask yourself whether it exists because it is hard to describe any other way or because it is a fantasy that comes from an unwillingness, conscious or otherwise, to live in that reality.

Hanif Kureishi suggested creativity was something that children did when their parents went out of the room. Other people have suggested that creativity is what parents do when their children are out of the room.

Fantasy is what you do when they are still in the room.

It may help to take a look at a literary example of understanding the myths and fantasies we create. Indeed, it was the inspiration for the title of this chapter.

When L. Frank Baum wrote *The Wizard of Oz*, he was writing about the possibility of growth through acceptance of yourself and who you are. He believed that this would be accomplished only if you appreciated that the powerful authority, the wizard, to whom we look for help, is just another struggling human being. When a group of unhappy people come to the wizard for answers, like a good psychotherapist he assigns them a task to do – as no matter how powerful he seems, he cannot do for them what they must do for themselves, or even tell them how to do it. The group insists that they are unable to do what they are asked to do, but the wizard does not let them off the hook.

When they get caught up in the task, they show genuine concern for one another and do what they were wishing they could do, without thinking, because it is for someone else.

As soon as we get released or release ourselves from the delusion that some magic is going to tell us or give us what we have wished for and fulfil our self-indulgent wish to have it right now, another possibility occurs: that we are our own authority, and other people can put us in touch with what is important in our lives.

Interestingly, when the group return to the wizard, having completed their task, they have not yet realized that what they seek they already have. In fact, when they learn that the wizard is not a "real" wizard, they are shocked to see he is "just a common man", and believing him to have deceived them they say he is "a very bad man".

The illusion of all-powerful is all theirs, not his. His illusion may be that he had to be a wizard in order for people to believe what he said. Maybe that isn't an illusion. Maybe that is how we are.

This particular group were ready to believe in him for as long as he had some "wizard" authority attached to him. He knew that as soon as they saw the man behind the curtain, their illusion would be shattered. If a so-called ordinary person was able to come up with answers, why hadn't they?

"But how can I help being a humbug, when all these people make me do things that everybody knows can't be done?"

That is why he says take no notice of the man behind the curtain, because in his illusion they will only believe him if he is the wizard, not an ordinary human being. He has ended up colluding with their illusion.

However, if he had told them right from the moment they came to see him that they already had the abilities to do what they wanted, would they have believed him? Probably not. The insights are so simple and obvious that maybe they can be seen only when an individual stops demanding someone else to do it for them.

We are often convinced that there is a really complex and magical solution; maybe because then we cannot be considered capable of doing it. We create our own illusions and fantasies. If we don't want to believe that reality is behind the curtain, we will create an illusion, wizard or otherwise.

the big difference

momentum

Unbearable reality

We can also feel that life without illusions would be unbearable. This is when we get drawn to the magnet of our own drama; sometimes to the point of addiction. Sometimes it feels hard to admit that we are ordinary people living in a world with no special plans....The magnet of the drama of your own experience...we become addicted to the drama, then use the drama to avoid the moment. We always make the drama external to us. The drama gets the adrenalin going, and when it does that, it's really difficult to stop. Fight or flight; it narrows decision pathways. Even if you can be convincing at this point, you are unlikely to be authentic. For some people, the worst thing you could say to them would be that they were mediocre or normal.

Sharon was having a hard time at work accepting that her performance over the past year had not been up to her or her boss's expectations. In order to avoid facing up to it, she used a real-life event – someone in her family who was very ill – as a means of changing the focus of attention from people disapproving of her to people feeling sorry for her and wanting to support her. She dramatized both the circumstances of the event and its effect on her to make her "story" more "interesting". (In her perception; her fantasy is based on the fact that she herself could not be interesting enough to merit the attention of others except in a negative way.)

The assumption she was making was that people saw her poor performance as something they wanted to criticize her for and leave it at that. Of course, the irony is that they would have given her as much support to look at changing her performance as emotional support to deal with family distress. Her fantasy was that sickness was more dramatic and therefore more attractive. It made her more special.

Escaping yourself to deal with things doesn't really make any sense, and yet that is what our defences get us to do.

In adolescence, we discover that life is not what children have been led to believe it would be. Suddenly nothing makes sense any more; the idea of growing up and having to lose our fantasies is overwhelming. Somehow we have to make life understandable, meaningful and manageable. How?

"The illusion of freedom is that it is getting away from things you don't like. I believe that freedom is working with what is."

Jerilyn Munyon

As children we are encouraged to try to be something other than ourselves, to meet someone else's expectations. We are told to assume a character, or live out a plot line that is given to us. Improvisation is usually unacceptable. People often miscast us in roles they would like to have themselves, or to fulfil their unfulfilled dreams....

There doesn't seem to be any way to get through the day without spending some part of it playing out temporary roles. We perform social, professional and personal actions that do not engage or reveal very much of who we really are. Sometimes we confuse the actor with the part or the self with the mask.

How much of this we choose to take on is part of doing what we'd rather be doing. In making the choice of what we would really like to do, we have to leave the fantasies out of it, otherwise we would never know whether we were doing what we'd rather be doing or acting out a fantasy......It doesn't mean never having any imagination, it means knowing when it is appropriate and when it isn't.

This means understanding what is behind our wild imaginings.

One way of doing this is looking at what we would physiologically call referred pain: the place in the body where the pain appears is not necessarily where the pain comes from. To take the pain away, you must therefore identify first what is causing the pain. As it is with the body, so it is in our emotional lives. We present one thing, but the real issues come from a different place.

Sometimes a fantasy can help understand what the real pain is for you. That means being able to describe it and the impacts, positive and negative, it has on you.

In order to understand what is real and what is fantasy, you need to identify what your thoughts, feelings and fantasies mean to you. Only to you. It is about what creates the fantasy for you, why it holds importance, and what it gives you.

So it isn't just about knowing what your wildest dreams are, it's also about understanding their importance to you. This is pretty much the difference between treating the symptoms of a disease and identifying and treating the cause. Doing the former may give you instant relief but is unlikely to prevent recurrence or cure. Doing the latter may take longer but is more likely to lead to a cure rather than a palliative.

Chris Argyris describes the difference between the two as single and double-loop thinking. The example he uses is one where if you were cold, single-loop thinking would lead you to turn up the thermostat on the heating. Double-loop thinking would ask a series of questions designed to find out what was behind you feeling cold. The response could be anything from you are suffering from a cold, the thermostat is broken, you are hungry, to the heating is not working or the outside temperature has dropped ten degrees, and so on. Without asking the questions, you may end up with a repeat of the same problem some time soon. If you are thinking in a single-loop mode, you see a problem and go about fixing what it is you see. In double-loop thinking, you ask what is creating this situation or problem and work to deal with that rather than what is presented.

In the spirit of a chapter about fantasy, let's return to metaphor.

Single loop is tip-of-the-iceberg thinking. Most of the iceberg is under water and hidden from sight. What you actually see is a warning of what might be below.

Accepting a myth or fantasy as it presents itself may not tell you the size or the nature of the issue you are dealing with. Without that knowledge, not only may you be dealing with the wrong problem you may also just be shuffling the deckchairs on the *Titanic*, so to speak.

"On the surface it seems deep."

Pauline Kael of the film *Gandhi*

take no notice of the man behind the curtain...

the big difference

momentum

Time out

This is a good spot to take a breather. Taking time to think doesn't slow down the process, in fact sometimes it speeds it up, or unblocks something. Fantasy is an intense subject to think about. Let your mind wander a bit.

"'A man without a mask' is indeed very rare. One even doubts the possibility of such a man. Everyone in some measure wears a mask, and there are many things we do not put ourselves into fully. In 'ordinary' life it seems hardly possible for it to be otherwise."

R.D. Laing

Michael walked out into the sunshine on the boat. He sat down and looked at the river. He lit his cigarette, inhaled deeply and carried on talking.

"I suppose the last time I felt truly confident about who I was and what I could be and wanted to be – the last time I truly *knew* me – was when I was 16. I was indestructible. Then, in a punishment unequal to the crime, I got thrown out of the system. This excluded me from everything – the rules I hated and the one thing I felt I was good at. I spent a couple of years trying to find a different way of living in the system, but I had lost my gyroscope for navigation. I think it was then that I realized my dream was over.

"With this illusion shattered and my confidence with it, I guess I lost me. I drifted into all sorts of things; some dangerous, some pleasurable, some both. I'm not even sure I can or could distinguish the two sometimes. I presented myself as someone who was laid back, mellow and capable of dealing with whatever came my way (which of course is basically true. However, it is missing the extra spark…)."

He paused for a second, and looked out over the river.

"My positive references all go back to my teens. I was, and still am to a lesser extent, stranded there, cut adrift. It's hard to live with confidence; I have been without it for so long. How do I get back to me? I have covered me with so much myth that I don't know where myth begins and reality ends. I don't know how to access me."

Michael spoke of his teen years with unbelievable enthusiasm, and a really strong sense of self. It was as if they were his touchstone. He did not know how they impacted on the choices he made as an adult. There were occasional flashes in his adult story which had the same spirit, but it was clear that he was touching this shore by accident, and not by dint of navigation.

At the age of 39, he felt he was in a similar position to when he was 19. He had been drifting for a while, and needed to, in his words, gird his loins for action. The difference was a greater awareness of how good he was at fooling himself and others about what he was like. He had in fact got a really clear idea of the things that were important to him, but was not sure how to live them, and what it would mean he would have to lose by giving up the myth. Was he ready to give it up?

take no notice of the man behind the curtain...

the big difference

momentum

Michael, like many of us, had at a deep level a strong sense of self, but didn't and doesn't know who he is and what he wants to be. Sounds a little paradoxical, but Michael says he understands the paradox. Deep down, he is very aware of the things that matter to him. Where it becomes hazy and confused is whether, and how, he can live a life that is true to these values, and attain the happiness and contentment he seeks. His fear is that he will never find it, and so he clings to his fantasies, thereby making sure that he never does …oops, there goes another paradox…

Some of his being seen as and perceiving himself to be special in his adolescence had left him in an idealistic search for an effortless, mystical triumph over life's practicalities. He hoped to find a way to stay high all the time, attaining spiritual and emotional growth without any great effort on his part. Because of his need to avoid making mistakes or risking failure, he either tried the extremes of hedonism or "hung out".

We build up people, places and things to be things they are not and could never be, both positive and negative.

We imbue people in our lives with qualities they do not have; we attribute to them behaviours they do not actually display; we hold them responsible for things which belong to us.

So what does this add up to?

the big difference

take no notice of the man behind the curtain...

A MASSIVE DELUSION CREATED BY

THE MAN BEHIND THE CURTAIN?

take no notice of the man behind the curtain....

the big difference

momentum

WE ARE THE MAN BEHIND THE CURTAIN; WE CREATE THE PROJECTIONS, THE MYTHS, AND THE LEGENDS.

So if we are the creators, how and why do we do it?

Our projections, myths and legends come from all sorts of diverse places. Every society has its way of keeping fantasies alive in us:

◆ the telling of fairy tales and stories in various media;

◆ our families;

◆ films;

◆ books;

◆ news stories;

◆ music;

◆ friends.

Sometimes we can even learn about what we fear from the films, plays, books or other people we don't like. Some are real incidents that we mythologize. Some are wished for or afear'd outcomes. Some are someone else's fantasies.

There is nothing wrong with fantasy in itself. It's when we entangle it with reality that it becomes hard for us to know what we want, what we have and what is real. All of us will have been absorbed in a book, film or piece of music at some time. It is interesting to understand what draws us to some fantasies, and what is unattractive about others.

Remaining aware of fantasies helps, but that's not always possible; deeply held fantasies are not always in our conscious mind.

Occasionally having a picture of a world where all events have a personal meaning provides us with the illusion of control. "These things are meant to happen and I know that..."

The story of *Alice in Wonderland* is a great metaphor for searching for meaning in a world which seemingly has none. Just like us, when surrounded by unfamiliarity Alice tries to make sense of things by using familiar structures such as multiplication tables and curtsying. All her everyday assumptions seem like empty illusions; all familiar ideas no longer have their old logic, and if she tries to apply the old logic, it leads her to incorrect conclusions.

the big difference

momentum

It almost seems as though the fantasy world is as unfair as the real world…..This would be a real nightmare; where the world you create to escape from your fears becomes as or more frightening.

So let's say you are living in a world where your fantasy is being very rich and successful. If it actually happens, your fantasy becomes real, and it isn't what you want in the real world; you are likely to be confused….It seems as though this is because in deciding what you wanted to achieve, you have omitted to ask the double-loop question about what would be important to you in achieving it. Without having asked this question you are seeking a fantasy that may be yours, or someone else's. It is still a fantasy, with everything that implies. Either way, it is unlikely to bring you what you wanted, because you didn't actually know what that was in the first place…

Living in a world that is not constrained by conventional wisdom means that we have the freedom to do as we please. That isn't always what we want. Sometimes we try to apply conventional wisdom to the fantasy, if it really isn't a pipe dream of our own.

That freedom is hard to hold on to. It means that we have to trust ourselves even when everyone around us seems to think that we don't know what we are doing. This can be problematic, particularly if we are not sure.

So the world of fantasy can be delusional and unconstructively unreal as well as exciting and fun. Some are happy to live their lives as a fiction, and can do so. Some are mad. Neurotics build castles in the air; psychotics walk in. Does that make Don Quixote a psychotic? Does it matter?

Well, it does if you want to knowingly make choices. Maybe it helps if you are truly delusional, because you then believe whatever it is you want to believe and live your life that way. The delusion may have happened as a defence against reality, but it has become your reality. There are many who live out delusions, though perhaps not to the extreme of Joan of Arc, but all of us are capable of delusion on a small scale. "I will be the one to change him." "I am the only one who can do this properly."

The question for you, dear reader, is whether the fantasy will inhibit you from doing what you'd rather be doing.

Oh, would that someone had all the answers for us...

The fantasy that some guru exists with all the answers gets played out both personally and professionally. No matter how much information we accumulate, however insightful and helpful, we are still saddled with the decision of what we actually do with the information.

"I've read all the books, seen the videos, travelled around and talked to people. I am still not content. I am not doing what I want to do. I am not happy. I need the answer.

Do you mean to tell me that all there is, is me? I have spent 20 years searching and that is what I end up with?"

Anonymous

No wonder we prefer a fantasy...

An imperfect solution

A curious person learns how the physical/social world works. This understanding helps to anticipate and manage the environment more closely. An individual who is very self-conscious is overly aware of the disparities between their ideal world and their actual one, and their life becomes somehow fitting the imperfect person into the imperfect world.

On one hand, to make a choice, to know what you really want, you need to abandon the idealized version of how life should work. It is also important to learn to make room in life for chance and imagination.

We have always been reliant on our imagination to create form and order in an otherwise ambiguous, frustrating and indifferent world. We often choose to fool ourselves. Some illusions are sanctioned as play and creativity, others perceived as delusional madness.

Knowing and differentiating is the hard part.

Unlike many books, there is no finite resolution of life's rich tapestry, apart from dying (and many believe that that is not the end either).

Most stories have a beginning, middle and end. It would be unusual for us to know at any given time where we are in our story. There are defined good guys and bad guys. In life, these tend to merge and fade into each other.......

Most drama and fiction also takes out the unbearable ordinariness of being, which for many of us constitutes a large part of our lives. Sometimes living with that itself is enough for us to create fantasies.

Children's freedom of thought comes from a desire to know. It also comes from not caring, from caring too much, from feeling cared for and from looking for a way to be cared for and not hurt. We still harbour these emotions. When they are embedded in fantasies, they are hard to manage.

Doing what you would rather be doing is dependent on you focusing on the desire to know and understand, rather than the desire to protect and defend.

The real excitement of living your life is to accept this and live. Not to expect to know what comes next. To know when the fantasies are helpful and exciting and when they will stop you making a difference.

"CHERISH YOUR OWN EMOTIONS

AND NEVER UNDERVALUE THEM."

Robert Henri

take no notice of the man behind the curtain...

the big difference

momentum

stuck

stuck

We are presented with opportunities in life; we frequently ignore them, or choose not to take them. It is not that we don't have the opportunities, we just don't take them. We often go for options which we know will get us into trouble, or if not trouble are not necessarily what we want. The jobs you take that aren't what you want; the extra work you keep taking on; the bullying boss you keep submitting to.....

What is up with that?

What is so attractive about **not** doing what you would rather be doing that you do it? We have all sorts of traps, addictions, and rituals that seem far more attractive to us than choosing what we really want to do.

Maybe it isn't that too much is not enough. It is that in order to have what we want, we first have to overcome the supreme hurdle of being honest with ourselves. All the elaborate plots we weave seem to center around pretence and deceit. This chapter looks at some of the ways we keep ourselves stuck. Without acknowledging them, we are doomed to wade in their treacle for ever.

"There are mighty few people who think what they think they think."

Robert Henri

Drama

"It was the boredom that comes of being cut off from everything that could make life sweet, or arouse curiosity, or enlarge the range of the senses. It was the boredom that comes of having to perform endless tasks that have no saviour and require skills we would gladly be without."

Robertson Davies, *Fifth Business*

This is the antithesis of "I'm doing what I'd rather be doing" – what makes us keep doing things that we find tedious?

It looks dull, but what does it take to move something from being dull to being toxic? It seems to happen to us without us realizing; something we have "abided" for a while suddenly becomes unbearable. What happens to change its effect?

Is this when we become addicted to the drama of our lives, and find it hard to accept life without drama? Is it when we feel ourselves to be "boring" in comparison to our friends?

"I warned my therapist that sometimes I do things or make choices in order to make the story more interesting."

Anonymous

It is so much more compelling to listen to drama than data…Even when we tell the dramatized stories, they never feel like lies; maybe more like shorthand for a less satisfying truth. In being diverted by the drama, we sometimes miss what Armistead Maupin called the "unscripted intrigues of everyday life".

The problem of course is we become hypnotized and trapped by the dramatic world, to the point where we are bound to be disappointed with the real world. Nothing there could meet our expectations as we have been seduced by a dramatic world. Nothing can compete with our imagination, or our need to make the world and ourselves more exciting, mysterious and funnier than they really are. Trapped in our own unreality.

Nina had long sought the perfect relationship. When "it" finally presented itself she convinced herself that despite all the major obstacles it was throwing up, and the alarm bells that were going off in her head, she was not going to lose the opportunity to have her dream come true. When put like that, who would want to miss a dream coming true? However, if the dream was based on completely unreal expectations, someone was going to end up crying.

Nina was able to create a totally plausible range of logical arguments and rationale for behaviours which to everyone else seemed like ingesting a slow acting poison. Being without the drama of an unpleasant situation became an unacceptable outcome for her, however sick it was making her.

"She's a victim of her senses, do you know her?"

Neil Young

It certainly is easier to see things when they are exciting and dramatic, whether the drama is positive or negative. Once the adrenalin starts to flow, it is hard to stop it. You become so wired that it's really hard to see what is happening. Then the next time, it is the adrenalin excitement which becomes the draw, and without that, life seems disappointing. All adrenalin makes choice out of the question. By the time that stuff is coursing through your veins, you are more than ready to roll. Too much and you get so anxious that your heart beats faster and you produce yet more, making you even more anxious and out of breath. You do need a little adrenalin in order to get excited enough to face the danger you perceive. Of course, if we took the time out to choose everything, we would drive ourselves nuts. Part of life's rich tapestry, and indeed the things that help us choose, is living some things as they happen, and occasionally going with the adrenalin.

"If you were happy every day of your life, you wouldn't be a human being. You'd be a game show host."

Veronica in *Heathers*

In relationships many people are more inspired by the chase than the actual relationship and so find staying in one very uninspiring and dissatisfying. When on adrenalin and excitement it is easy to be convincing, both to yourself and to others, but hard to be authentic.

Sometimes we believe ourselves to be totally uninteresting and thence unworthy without the drama.

It is just as easy to get caught up in the drama of work. Here the drama is often to do with making life totally unlivable for yourself. Making a story over-dramatic in order to be heard stops us seeing the reality. For example, at work this may be the fact that we are unhappy in our jobs but are too lacking in confidence to think that we could get work somewhere else. Joe, whom we have heard from before, was a long-term veteran of his organization: 15 years. Many of his colleagues talked in the same way; they spoke of things happening to them, and being powerless to do anything about it.

The "stuck" in these situations seems to me to be the fear of leaving. If you are that unhappy, why would you stay, unless you were more comfortable being unhappy, or you were scared of the unknown outside? (Whatever the outside might be...)

"This week everything went wrong. People were horrible to me. I didn't seem to have any space for myself. The only bright spot was when I had to go and work with an external supplier. That was really productive. I need a day off. Am I going nuts? I refuse to let it get to me, and I'm really annoyed. Now I feel as though I have let them get to me and I feel stressed."

Joe needed to matter more to himself than the people at work mattered to him. He even felt that he could not take a day off sick as he had too much to do.

Joe will not be able to unstick himself until he recognizes he is stuck. He then needs to want to try something new.

These are big leaps and sometimes the "victim drama" of the unpleasant situation is more attractive to deal with than newness and accountability.

Drama is about contending with complex and often contradictory forces. It is also a way to investigate the complexity of our situation. Drama is different to propaganda, which employs any means necessary to persuade us to accept an agenda of dogma and foregone conclusions. We can be so good at creating and falling for our own propaganda.

"I have argued quite eloquently."

Jonathan Ross

"You haven't stopped talking, that's not the same."

Paul Merton *Room 101*

It isn't just mumbling the words of understanding and getting the concept. That is part of the way there, but it's also a way of deluding yourself that you **are** there. It's another way to stay stuck, to be able to articulate without being able to do.

If you want to be doing what you would rather be doing, it isn't a case of choice good, everything else bad, it is about knowing when the path you are taking will get you what you want. Are the things you are doing going to get you stuck or free you?

There is no doubt that tensions can move people, they don't have to keep them stuck. However, sometimes if you surface problems without context, people do not move on, they freeze in their tracks. If you get too worried about what you are saying or doing, you are not conscious of what you are saying or doing, only of the worry. Therefore you may well commit the heinous crime you are frightened of….deer frozen in the headlights.

Coming unstuck

Unsticking is about separating the problem from the anxiety.

It is about knowing what the situation is, and knowing what it is about the situation that concerns you. When you are trying to work out what to do in a situation, try separating the things that make you anxious from the situation. It can be very revealing.

This has to happen before the worry turns into blind panic and stops you being able to see or feel anything except the worry.

Eric had held a senior management job successfully for four years. When he restructured his division as the company expanded, his job grew. This should have been a moment for him to take stock and look to see how he was going to have to manage differently, but the panic of having to be immediately successful took over.

His boss was charismatic, sensitive and given to spontaneous decision making. They had had a great relationship and he trusted Eric's ability, while Eric trusted his judgement. Eric had been in the new job for three weeks when he started to get stressed. He was snapping at people for no reason and getting migraines. He was missing small deadlines. His boss started to question what was going on, and instead of seeing it as a reasonable question, Eric saw it as a loss of faith, and immediately raised his anxiety level from medium to off the scale. As soon as his anxiety level went up, his behaviour became more erratic and the very behaviour he was hoping to avoid – that is, disapproval from his boss – happened.

Eric put it down to his boss having no faith in him, and losing trust. He wanted a showdown with his boss to challenge him. When asked what he would like his boss to do differently, he remained silent for some time, and eventually replied that he didn't know.

Eric had confused his anxiety – to be seen to be doing a good job – with the problem – working out how he would have to behave differently to be successful in the job. As soon as he got locked in this anxiety state, he had to find someone to blame, so he aimed everything at his boss (who of course had some culpability, but we are good at finding plausible people to blame; in that way we get to blame them for longer).

Separating out the anxiety from the problem means checking out your intent about the situation: that is, knowing what you want to achieve by the actions you are taking. Surprisingly, we rarely ask ourselves this simple question: what do I hope to achieve by doing that? Try it, it gets you a lot of perspective. While you are at it, try these questions too:

What is it you would like to see happen differently?

What would you like others to be doing differently?

What would you see yourself doing differently?

"The hardest thing to see
is what is in front of your eyes."

Johann Wolfgang von Goethe

Why was it so hard for Eric to admit he was anxious or unhappy?

"Are you unhappy?"
"Not inordinately so."

Two characters in *Psycho*

Well what does that mean?

One of the things we seem terrified to do is to admit we are unhappy or happy, so we qualify everything. And just like having a company audit that is "qualified", it means little or nothing, to both the speaker and the listener. Inordinately. Inordinate to what? Whose measure do we use, if any? Why is it so hard to say yes I am happy or no I am not?

Commitment is a pretty crucial part of making a difference; a qualified desire doesn't really count. Okay, it does not count.

It seems so hard to shift from wherever we are to something new; and the desire to stay with what we know, rather than the unknown, is so powerful that we will stick with things we don't actually like, rather than risk the new. At least with the familiar we know what will happen, even if it's bad. If it's bad, we know what it will feel like, and sometimes that is easier than something new.

Attraction and repulsion – we can immobilize ourselves with our confusion – we frequently do. That immobilization is so painful that we take a route, any route, so as not to feel the pain of immobilization. It seems to give us the illusion of reasserting control. Sometimes the route out is inertia itself, usually accompanied by the myth that we are just rolling with it.

Inertia or even the prison of procrastination.

You have brains in your head, and feet in your shoes. Why is it so hard sometimes to decide where to go?

Sometimes we are fatalistic and avoid going in any defined direction, fearing that the focus will shut out other chances. So we base our ambitions on what others have done or expect of us.

Well, you don't move at all sometimes. And when you're in a slump, getting yourself out is not the easiest of tasks.

You may end up in a place you don't recognize, with no visible street markings or familiar landmarks.

"Simple it's not, I'm afraid you will find, for a mind-maker-upper to make up his mind."

Dr Seuss

There are some things that will scare you so much that you won't feel able to go on. Then there is what Dr Seuss called the Waiting Space.

"… waiting around for a Yes or No
or waiting for their hair to grow.
………or a Better Break
or a string of pearls, or a pair of pants
or a wig with curls, or Another Chance."

Waiting has such a negative connotation for us. Whether it is having to wait in a coffee shop, or being seen to be waiting for something, it has no positive connotation. This is not true in all cultures however. We seem to connect waiting with being indolent or inactive. Waiting for time can become something we anticipate having or coming rather than worrying about having to make time. However, it does give us a marvellous excuse to do something/anything......and if it is wrong, we have something to blame.

"I can't think about this now. I'll go crazy if I do. I'll think about it tomorrow. After all, tomorrow is another day."

Scarlett O'Hara

The truth, the whole truth, and everything but the truth

There is a standard flow of troubleshooting we get into:

We find a problem; we deny it; we get around it.

And what is wrong with that, I hear you ask. Well nothing, if it gets you to do what you want to do. If it does, then you are doing what you'd rather be doing. If it doesn't, then it is time to ask the question about whether you want things to be different.

If you can picture yourself at a fork in the road. On the one hand is a road that takes you somewhere you have never been, you have no clue what is down that road, whether it will be easy or hard for you. It is where you "want" to go.

The other road is a road you are familiar with. You know where it goes to, where the bends are, and all the scenery en route. It is not where you "want" to go.

In terms of doing what you would rather be doing, it doesn't matter which road you choose, as long as you do so knowingly, or as the Californians would say, choicefully.

Knowingly means you can go down the road accepting that it will not change anything in your life and stay there. You may do so because you know it is not what you want, and you admit you don't feel able to cope with the uncertainty of change. Or you may take the unknown road that has no certainty for you, and holds out the possibility of new and exciting. It also holds the possibility of failure. Knowingly means that you accept the fact that it is unknown, and therefore renounce expectation of what might happen.

The key word in both of those paths is acceptance. In terms of making a Big Difference, if you **ACCEPT** the path you have chosen, then you are free and are doing what you'd rather be doing, even if it means standing still.

However, being accountable for that decision is what drives people to assume there is another path. Indeed, they think they see one down the middle of the other paths. This is a path that says, well, I know I should be, but, it's too hard, and there must be something else, which I will surely stumble upon if I just keep going. This is an illusory path; it is more like the paths that you come across in Scottish peat bogs. They start off with a seeming purpose, then peter out and you are left in the middle of nowhere, wondering how you got there and what to do next.

The peat bog option is most people's preferred option.

I am sure you will have recognized it as a seemingly attractive option that you will have travelled on many a time. It puts off action, denies commitment and ensures that you don't have to face any of your demons. It does feel like you are at least moving, but because you have not made an active choice, you are never free or comfortable, and the movement is illusory; temporary at best. So the big trap here is our lack of honesty with ourselves.

One of the key things that keeps us stuck is our lack of honesty with self and others. Using that word is incredibly emotive. Few people like the thought of being dishonest (with self or others). They can at a pinch respond to not being "honest with myself", but not dishonest. Yet that is what we often are, deliberately or not, consciously or unconsciously.

We tell ourselves we are quite happy with drifting/whatever and then say we are not. So little time, yet we waste it on dishonest relationships, doing things we don't want to do.

"You scream and shout, you make a scene;
when you open your mouth,
you never say what you mean..."

Lucinda Williams

Maybe there is no absolute truth, and drama is just one way of expressing it.

stuck

the big difference

momentum

MAYBE EVERYTHING IS TRUE,

SOMETIMES.

the big difference

momentum

Everyone lies, cheats, pretends. When you succeed in deceiving others, you are left isolated and unknown.

All images of self are incomplete.

Most of us are not all we claim to be.

Few of us are who we were taught we were supposed to be.

So in the spirit of making a difference:

the trap is to stay dishonest; the risk is not knowing what will happen; and the prize is freedom: being accountable for who you are.

At this point, I can offer no how to's (as if I would...)

Being honest means being honest. You either are or you aren't. We are a short time on the planet, and it does seem to be an awful waste of time to lie to oneself. Your call.

While you ponder the wide open spaces of coming to terms with yourself, here are a few other devices we use to keep ourselves stuck.

Toxic waste

Poisonous: any substance which taken into or formed in the body destroys life or impairs health; any malignant influence.

What's the attraction with toxic? Sometimes it seems we are attracted to things that we don't have, which can harm, might harm, do harm.......

We can walk away or stay.

Suzanne spent ten years in a relationship which she knew to be "toxic". She and her partner found they were genuinely attracted to each other, but the unspoken conditions of the relationship meant that she bossed around and he submitted. It suited both of them to have someone to blame for their dissatisfaction with their lives. When it finally blew up and they separated, both of them were at loss to know how to live without their "victim" status. Living without blame was a new experience. One dived straight into another relationship, the other became very depressed. Both felt lost. The toxins had held them together; unhappy, but together. The price they paid for together was misery and repression. Would they do it again? Probably. The familiarity would be very tempting. We don't always learn from our experience; mistakes or otherwise.

"I have a strong sense of self-control."
"What makes you lose it?"
"Tequila does it."

Overheard conversation

Sandy listlessly leafed through the pile of magazines on her couch. The sun was shining through her window, but she was not sure she wanted to be out in it on her own. She sighed.

"I spend my time problem solving for others. I love my job, but it takes me away from a stable home life. It is easy in one sense for me to do it, as my kids are grown up and I have no primary relationship to manage. Although my work means I am constantly working with ambiguity and spontaneity, I also have to plan my life, so that I am in the places I need to be at the appropriate time. This leaves me starving for emotional spontaneity and excitement. I think I have looked for that in relationships which have the potential to be toxic. The attraction to people who are emotionally exciting fuels my emotional energy, but does not make me feel safe. Safety or excitement? Can I have both? Are the two mutually exclusive?"

Does she have to choose?

I guess you could argue that it depends on definition, but that's a cop out. I wonder what is missing in Sandy that she feels the need for safety and excitement outside of herself. Does she get it from her job and therefore any relationship would be found wanting, because of the everyday ordinariness of being?

Fascination. Fascinated by something different.

How different does something have to be before it becomes toxic?

Chances are we may replicate the same interactions at work and in relationships; for example, if we choose to be in a relationship where we are submissive to a parental figure, we may well do the same at work.

"I had a highly toxic boss once and the end result was that I was left feeling very low, doubting my own abilities and god knows why I stayed there 18 months – that was a year too long…I was stuck."

Without knowing the data in this situation it would be hard to understand what kept this person stuck. God may know why she stayed there 18 months, but she probably does too. She just hasn't asked the questions.

Unsticking means asking the questions. Discussing the undiscussables.

"My egotism frightens me. There is a spectator in me who watches…for whom everything is puppetry, even – and especially – me!"

Jacques-Henri Lartigue

Sometimes the attraction is to do with a survival mechanism you don't appear to have, for example people who have survived, literally, difficult situations. There is something in the belief that we too might survive if we hang out with this person.

Jonathan was drawn to saving souls. The more poisoned the better. He felt he could be the antidote they had never known, and he could clear the poison from their system. He did this at work and in his personal life. He loved the struggle and the suffering. Others may not know it, but they were desperately in need of him. He alone could right the wrongs of an unjust world. (Sick windmills are my game….)

So what was his intent in clearing the poison? What poison did he have in his own system?

Takes on things that belong to others. Or give yourself away…What would it be like to sit with your own discomfort, or that of others, without trying to hide from it, diminish it, or fix it?

Jonathan says he finds people to be the antidote to his own toxins. The problem is that his antidote lies outside himself, and whenever you introduce an outside element, you run the risk of bringing in another infection that you didn't bargain for. This metaphor gets overly complicated at this point, so to sum it up, in looking to other people to cure ourselves, we bring other issues into the system.

"All swindlers on earth are as nothing to the self-swindlers."

Charles Dickens, *Great Expectations*

Andrew was more drawn to the physically toxic. At 35, after a successful career as a trader in investment banking, he had everything material he had ever wanted. He had reached a point in his life when he thought, is that all there is? I don't know what else to strive for. He could have gone travelling, bought a motorbike, taken up BASE jumping, and any number of things. What he ended up doing was immersing himself in another scene where he could

stuck

the big difference

momentum

indulge his acquired habit of living fast and on a constant high. Except he chose an artificial stimulant. It achieved the desired effect, but he found himself as stuck in that way of being as he had felt previously. Nothing had really changed. He had swapped one addiction for another, and was as stuck as he had ever been.

"Making friends wasn't a problem. I'm the kind of person people are drawn to. But because of that I am easily influenced. I like to feel good and to feel part of something really exciting. I would probably have been comfortable without sex drugs and rock 'n' roll. It could have been anything. It's just that it was there. If stuff falls into your lap, it's hard to say no – particularly if you have no alternative in mind, and people are watching you and expecting something, anything…"

Toxicity may not be only things which are physically dangerous. Things which can harm our body and spirit often reside in our ability to block things which can create "toxic" situations. Or what Chris Argyris calls common social virtues.

We use helpful-sounding words such as support, respect and team play and create unreal situations that do not reflect the truth of feelings.

What are you pretending not to know?

For example, we say what we think other people want to hear. We don't challenge others' thinking processes that we believe have rendered a subject undiscussable. We say one thing and think the opposite. Our actions and non-verbal communication tend to be more in line with what we don't say than with the words that come out of our mouths.

I guess we can fool some of the people some of the time….We maintain the appearance of working together, and do not challenge what others do, except in our heads. Then we wonder why things seem to always turn out the same way.

We all consider ourselves honest, and yet when it comes to telling the truth as we feel it, we are pitiful. We mask it by saying we don't want to "hurt" others, and then go ahead and hurt them by our dishonesty. This doesn't make much sense to me, particularly if you hear yourself say, "I just wish you'd tell me the truth…"

This level of dishonesty creates toxins in the system which if left unchecked can certainly prove deleterious to self and others.

At the root of those behaviours however is the level of awareness of your behaviour and impact on a situation or person(s). How acknowledging are you of your behaviour and its impact on both the person and the situation? How knowledgeable are you?

Most films that you watch will rely on your assumptions to lead you somewhere so that the script can then surprise you, in whatever dramatic way the film requires. In real life, we not only create assumptions about others, we have them about ourselves, and rarely check ourselves out. We then wonder why we usually end up in the same place. The same capacity that we use to make sense of ambiguous clues can become so rigid and inflexible that the clues become meaningless or unacceptable, or both.

"Technique is more than anything else a means of evading the personally impossible, of disguising a deficiency."

Graham Greene

All of Greene's novels focus around a character's "deficiency", that is, something that they are lacking. We can build whole personalities around the disguise of the deficiency, to the point where the technique has become an end in itself obscuring the deficiency it was hiding. That's why it is so hard sometimes to answer the question about what your weaknesses are. If you have spent many years denying your deficiencies, why should you suddenly have any in response to a question?

It's like hitting yourself with a brick and then justifying it by saying that it was just a small brick.

So in life we are capable of developing "techniques", which could mean anything from incredible expertise or skill in something, or remarkably sophisticated defence mechanisms, which disguise the things we are "deficient" in. Disguising the deficiency means we don't ever try to improve it or work it into our lives. It kind of implies that deficiency is a weakness as opposed to something that either is or can be improved. It does mean that we focus on developing the techniques rather than living with the deficiency.

the big difference

momentum

Your deficiency could be anything from an over-reliance on your intuition (therefore you lack the desire to check things out) to an irrational need to be right all the time (therefore you lack the ability to be wrong). Without knowing what your deficiency/ies is/are, you have no idea of your boundaries. Neither can you have any idea of what you are capable of, or what would constitute a risk for you.

It is hard to own up to deficiencies,

unless you see it as a positive option. That means fighting against the many messages, liminal and subliminal, that tell us that deficiency is bad. It may not be how we want to be, but that doesn't make it "bad". It is a piece of us. Keeping deficiencies as "bad" prevents you from working with you. So first you have to change that mental model that has it as not OK to have or own up to deficiencies. There is, of course, the distinct possibility that you may not even be able to get rid of them all…..

So know them and their impact. Then decide what you want to do about them.

Our awareness of ourselves and others is fraught with assumptions that often lead to errors in the manner in which we consider the way things appear, and the way we think. We are usually, but not always, aware of our intentions, but less aware of how we actually act or are perceived.

So I can see what is in my way, and what I want to do, but I cannot see how I act that out or the effect that I have on you internally. We are more aware of other people's actions, and their effect on self, at least. We may think we know what other's intentions are, but we are often wrong. If we are often unaware of what is behind our actions, this is even more so for our knowledge of what is behind other people's actions.

PHEW. Still there?

So I can see what you do, and the effect you have on me, but I can't see what is in your way, or what you are trying to do.

"You should say what you mean," the March Hare went on.
"I do," Alice hastily replied, "at least, I mean what I say – that's the same thing you know."
"Not the same thing a bit!" said the Hatter.

Lewis Carroll, Alice in Wonderland

The end result of this blind world is that we often see ourselves as doing "the right thing", but obstructed by other people and the situation. In this way we make others the source and cause of the problem (and of course, the center of the universe) and find it hard to see our contribution. That makes it hard for us to come up with ways of choosing what *we* can do differently if we only perceive others as our obstacles.

We are also capable of demonizing these "obstacles".

"Life is pain, Highness. Anyone who says differently is selling something."

The Princess Bride

Another way of looking at this is to see others not as obstacles but as ways of checking, clarifying and enhancing our perceptions.

Then of course you lose the opportunity to blame someone or something else.... You also end up accountable....Ready for that?

Open secret....

Another way we hide from ourselves is by the use of secrets either about ourselves or about others.

"Everybody has something to conceal."

Sam Spade

Of course that's true. Why on earth would we tell absolutely everything about us? Who would really want to know? Using secrets as a way of withholding or controlling is another matter.

Sometimes we use them as currency to barter for something we want, to make us seem more powerful than another, to control a situation or individual or to create a myth or drama. We are usually seduced by being "trusted" with a secret. We like the pressure of keeping them, and the power of withholding.

They are also a great way to stay stuck. Sorry, can't tell you why because then I would have to kill you......

The 3 Rs: rebellion, revenge and resentment

Another tool in the treacle armoury is the 3 Rs. They keep you stuck because they are all dependent on there being someone else to blame. For as long as the perpetrator is external to you, you can do nothing. That is why they are such a good avoidance mechanism.

The 3 Rs cannot help you make any difference, let alone a Big One. They are grounded in the past.

"This is the revenge of the unlived life, Ramsay. Suddenly it makes a fool of you."

Robertson Davies, *Fifth Business*

Benjamin Pratt describes resentment as rusty swords that people keep in cupboards. When they pull them out, they hurt only themselves. An over developed sense of vengeance rarely leaves us satisfied, even in the unlikely event that we "get someone back".

"What are you rebelling against?"
"What have you got?"

Marlon Brando in *The Wild One*

Out of control

At the center for most of these stuck patterns of behaviour is a flawed desire to control what happens. Flawed because you can't.

Controlling doesn't let you do what you'd rather be doing. It merely stops what you perceive to be bad things from happening. It rarely creates or inspires.

We tend to either assume control or hand over control; often a mixture of the two. Of course, the irony is that the tighter you hold on, the less control you have. If you feel the need to hold on you are effectively saying that there is something out there which has more control than I do, so I had better hold on so that they can't control me. See the paradox? The only way to be in control is to let go.

Sometimes behaviours begin as coping mechanisms or rituals which were necessary to help us survive or work through something. Everyone has history.

The way we express it in the present may govern our ability to move away from it.

> Steve had a troubled youth. He spent a great deal of time watching people argue, get upset and hurt each other. To escape the pain that caused him, he created a world where everything was OK. He sees good everywhere. The world is good. Everything is good. In this way, he cannot be hurt. It does prevent him from dealing with conflict and making difficult decisions. But there is no denying that it helps him cope.

> In contrast, Barbara also came from a troubled youth, and she copes by creating a world where nothing is more or less important, so she feels able to cope with anything, as everything is the same.

In both cases, the rage is there. In Barbara it comes out as depression, in Steve it comes out as explosive bursts of uncontrolled anger. It's just like a corset; if you push or squeeze something into one place, it oozes out somewhere else.

Occasionally these coping strategies become a part of what we do, even when the crisis has passed. Ritual is a very useful piece of our safety mechanism, but like anything else, when used inappropriately, it distorts a situation and consequently our ability to see and respond in a constructive way. The rituals become a safety in themselves. Our fear becomes that if we stop the ritual, we become unsafe.

Diana had been a senior nurse in casualty for ten years. She said it was so hard to calibrate feelings in the emergency rooms that she had various rituals she observed to get her through the work she ultimately enjoyed. In front of the casualty area was a large screen. Initially, every day when she came on duty, she used to put her hands on the screen and say to herself, "Leave your feelings out here in the hall". After a while, she found she didn't need to put her hands on the screen, but her mind automatically spoke the words. So successful was this tactic that she found herself using the same approach in other parts of her life.

"I think I did that for years in my first marriage. I left my feelings out in the hall."

The ritual had helped her in a very practical way. She had also transferred the principle to another situation where it helped her to cope with a situation, but not deal with it. Once we develop a dependency on rituals, we look for them in many walks of our lives: action plans for careers, lists, tight goals and objectives, absolute methodologies, gurus with a message…

They are not damaging to us, but they will, by their nature, keep us from doing what we'd rather be doing. Unless, of course, we purposefully decide that we are going to adopt rituals as a way of being in the world, and accept the limitations that brings. That is a possibility, but coming out into the open with defence mechanisms lowers their protection value.

Know your poisons.

So we adopt all these methods of holding on.

What sort of things happen to us if we try to let go?

When frightened, we tend to freeze up. We lock ourselves up physically. (Yup, we still want to stay in control; we haven't really let go in our hearts and our heads.) When we are relaxed, we walk freely and our arms swing in opposition to each other. When we are afraid, our arms go to our sides, and when asked to swing or relax, we stiffen up completely. We rarely know this, and when someone tells us, the instinctive response is to deny it, as we are full of fear.... The isolation of fear means we don't move in relation to space or people, whether that is a physical or a psychological move.

Letting go means accepting the energy that you are getting from the outside world. One actor likened this feeling to the freeze that most actors feel before they go on stage. He said he felt very small, and the only way he could feel "big enough" to face the audience was to open his arms. In this way he felt bigger. He felt he had to feel the audience energy before he could accept it and be there with it. By opening his arms he felt he was moving the crowd inside of him (thereby controlling them...but he had to let go first...).

In American football, they call the crowd the 13th man in the team. This team member is what inspires and moves the team to greater heights.

This may all sound a little fanciful in terms of dealing with your everyday fears. It is not very different. We all have an "audience" we are fearful of – fearful of rejection, lack of approval, doing the wrong thing – so we freeze up. If we can let go and accept them as being there, and not try to control them, we have a chance of using their energy and absorbing it for our use.

Saying relax doesn't do it

It is partly about changing what improv actors call status behavior.

Changing how you perceive the things or people you are trying not to be fearful of. Even your actions can denote status: we hold eye contact when we want to dominate someone, or when we look at someone we admire, but we break eye contact and take quick glances when we are feeling submissive. If you touch your mouth when you look at someone, you'll feel hesitant but will be perceived as "lowering" your status. If you hold your head still, people perceive "high" status. If you're aware you are keeping your head still, it actually makes you feel in control (try saying "Make my day" and move your head around … it doesn't have quite the same effect).

We try to please "higher status" people by ruining our posture and constricting our voices. Usually the person who is playing the higher status takes up the most space, and is most relaxed. Someone whose arms are tightly symmetrically folded may seem very controlled but……

Familiarity can breed both high and low status…some of us are better at playing high or low, but both attitudes are defensive.

How we see others is a huge key to the traps we set for ourselves. By casting another in a "higher status" role to us, we automatically hand over control. In doing that we give away our responsibility and accountability. Makes life much easier. So unless the other person happens to want to let you do what you would rather be doing, you don't get to do it. But then you do have someone to blame. Whereas if you take the chance and the risk yourself, you may not be prepared to take the failure.

Taking a risk means taking the possibility of failure.

It is not a risk without that possibility. Many a time in life, we say we are taking a risk, but we are not taking on the risk of failure and are devastated when things don't work out.

So getting unlocked is about:

Being comfortable with the space you are in, physical and mental;

Feeling that your status with others is either equal or higher.

(This does not necessarily mean you see everyone in their underwear; that may sometimes have the reverse effect.)

Even when we have experienced the power of letting go, and know what we can do, it is sometimes easy to keep ourselves in known situations. So we choose "audiences" we are comfortable with. When something goes wrong we blame situations or people who have intruded onto our "stage".

The novice freezes, the more experienced person goes to a sophisticated series of defence mechanisms. Neither wants to change or lose what they perceive to be control.

Improvisation theater is an interesting place to look for patterns of behavior, because being a good improviser means letting go, being in the moment and accepting what is happening around and responding directly to it, not holding on to preconceived notions of your own. Improvisers describe four key groups of defences.

Blocking

This defence is about staying the same, not being changed, maintaining the illusion of control, not being hit by the bus. You also minimize the transitions you may have to make by being negative. Sound familiar? Yes but…….

Cancelling

When in this mode, you dismantle whatever has been established. Nothing has been or can be achieved. You don't respond to others, you ignore both them and any suggestions they make. You might withhold information or not add to ideas. Sound familiar? What did you say?

Sidetracking

This avoids interaction by talking about things that are happening elsewhere or at another time. Change the subject, make a joke, gossip, waffle, be "clever", take the attention away from the situation, either to you or something else. Sound familiar? Did you want some coffee? Well I knew someone who…

Driving

Take control by setting clear directions for everyone else, and tell them what the story is. You are no longer relative to the people around you. Sound familiar? What I think you should do is….

Stopping this is all dependent on awareness.

One way to raise awareness is to write down all your mistakes or have someone do it for you. Then ask yourself to make the mistakes deliberately. Another way is to forbid yourself to do the very thing you know you have to do but feel you can't do. It is astonishing how quickly forbidden fruit becomes attractive.

Telling people who are afraid to touch each other that they are now forbidden to do so, allows the excitement to overcome the fear. Telling someone who has procrastinated over something that their time is up and they can no longer do what they were supposed to do seems to stir them into action. (It doesn't always work, but it's got to be worth a try.)

The key to these rather contrary behaviors is overcoming the fear. It is fear that creates all the stuck behaviors. Knowing what the fear is about helps an enormous amount but doesn't take the fear away. Sometimes the only thing that does take the fear away is experiencing what it is you are frightened of. That is hard, not impossible.

When you deal with fear, the way out is in.

Ironically, using the rituals can help if they are seen in a less compulsive way.

Hilary Austen suggests that looking behind the behaviors to the patterns and themes helps us work out a principle for dealing with them. A principle does not have the obsessive, compulsive, stifling qualities of a ritual. It is a way of being that is actionable, portable, personalizable and revisable. This means it is:

Portable – something that can be transferred from situation to situation.

Revisable – something that can be upgraded and adapted to new situations.

Personalizable – something that fits your character, and doesn't belong to anyone else.

Actionable – something that achieves a difference and connects to something concrete.

The stuckness can provide us with a way out. Acknowledging the traps and where they come from allows us to adapt the knowledge to another outcome other than being stuck. At that point you can have a choice. First you have to admit you are stuck. No, really admit it, not Yes, but…Then try these principles as a framework for designing your way out; they are not a solution, just a way to help you think about what you need to think about.

"Man's disquiet is all of his own making."

Marcus Aurelius

People tend to judge others through fear and ignorance. If you know and accept, you have no need to judge; either self or others.

FEAR CREATES OUR WEBS AND ULTIMATE PRISONS
OF DECEIT AND PRETENCE.

THEY STOP US BEING WHO WE ARE AND DOING
WHAT WE'D RATHER BE DOING.

FACING FEARS SUCKS. GET OVER IT.

"I know I'm better because I feel worse.
The nicer you are, the harder it gets.
The stronger I grow the weaker I feel.
You can't give it to me because I already have
it......... .
The more lost I become, the clearer it gets.
I'm feeling confused, I must be in the right place.
The worst part is knowing I can make it.
The safest places are the most dangerous."

Sheldon Kopp client

THERE ARE NO BAD GUYS OR GOOD GUYS; THERE'S ONLY US.

stuck

the big difference

momentum

"I've been freed from the self
that pretends to be someone,
and in becoming no one,
I begin to live.
It is worthwhile dying,
To find out what life is."

T.S. Eliot

living in chaotic space

"THINGS FALL APART
THE CENTER CANNOT HOLD,
MERE ANARCHY IS LOOSED UPON THE WORLD."

W. B. Yeats

living in chaotic space

Making the Big Difference means a sojourn in chaotic space: undergoing a time when things are not in order, in place, or in any way comfortable. We usually run a mile from situations like this, and/or try to impose order on them. Actually living in chaotic space is essential in order to move on. If we opt for premature solutionization, we are likely to end up not making any difference.

William Bridges referred to this space as the "neutral zone" and sometimes it can feel neutral in that it is neither one thing nor another. It can last a few hours, days, months or years, depending on the individual and the circumstances. Getting out of it usually involves acknowledging it is there before you can move on. (Some people love the feel of randomness, and so it could be what you would rather be doing....)

Chaotic space creates a collision between outer and inner worlds that produces a jarring that is potentially very disturbing. Walter Murch tells the story that describes the effect of this kind of displacement on bees.

"A beehive can apparently be moved two inches each night without disorienting the bees the next morning. Surprisingly, if it is moved two miles, the bees have no problem. They are forced by the displacement of their environment to re-orient their sense of direction, which they can do easily enough. But if the hive is moved two yards, the bees become fatally confused. The environment does not seem different to them, so they do not re-orient themselves, and as a result, they will not recognise their own hive when they return from foraging, hovering instead in the empty space where the hive used to be, while the hive itself sits just two yards away."

Walter Murch

Is this delusional denial behaviour? Can the bees really not see the new hive? Do they really not have the initiative to look slightly out of their direct line of vision or experience?

Does any of this behaviour sound familiar?

Only bees, they don't have the intelligence to do anything different. Well, every day I see people do just this.

They stay fixated in the same pattern of behaviour

because it's what they are used to doing, even though it takes them nowhere and makes them feel confused.

Jean was totally overwhelmed by her new job and the lack of support she felt. She was disoriented and confused. The company had changed her job only slightly, and moved her desk, but it was disorienting enough for her to feel unable to do her job. A headhunter called her and invited her for an interview with a new company. She got the job and joined a totally new environment, where she "regained" her confidence and returned to her former dynamic self.

How often do we wish, when faced with a new development – personal or professional – in our lives to just be able to go away or start anew? If we examine the situation, not a great deal has changed, but enough to disorient us. Starting anew seems easier than adjusting. Why is that?

When we come across things about ourselves that are uncomfortable or different, it can take us into almost a state of shock – where differences are so deep that ordinary assumptions are overthrown, particularly if panic can overcome irritation. When things are that different, we frequently cannot find words to describe our thoughts and feelings. This leads us into more anxiety and panic, yet I am sure we have all experienced something out of our ordinary life, such as a sunset, a view, a piece of music, that was so wonderful that we lacked the appropriate words to describe the experience. That does not throw us into panic.

"Other worlds contain fabulous monsters."

Mary Catherine Bateson

Welcome to chaotic space

"Time flies like an arrow, fruit flies like a banana."

Groucho Marx

Discovering new territory in ourselves is likely to put us in a place where we feel uncomfortable. We need to be able to contextualize things in new scenery, and contextualize ourselves as characters in the new scene.

"Like the blue sky, the self is a matter of understanding and experience."

Mary Catherine Bateson

Most of us are searching, consciously or unconsciously, for a degree of internal balance between ourselves and the outside world. If we become aware of a volcano within us, we often compensate by urging restraint. In the same way, those of us who hold a glacier within may urge some form of passionate abandon. The danger is that the glacial person in need of passionate abandon may apply restraint instead.

What methods do we have for dealing with our own glaciers and volcanoes? Where do we let off steam and where do we melt?

It is frequently at the edges of things that we learn more about the middle.

Ice and steam can reveal more about the nature of water than water alone ever could.

The right questions to ask are the tough ones, the ones you can't answer immediately. You often need someone to ask them for you.

Sometimes you need someone to play the role of Fifth Business.

Robertson Davies describes this as "those roles which, being neither those of Hero nor Heroine, Confidante nor Villain, but which were nonetheless essential to bring about recognition or denouement, were called the Fifth Business....The Player acting these parts was often referred to as Fifth Business."

So sometimes we need to get someone else to ask the questions that help us find our way through chaotic space. It may not be a primary character in our lives. It might be someone you meet on a plane. You may be or have been Fifth Business for someone else.

It is an interesting notion that a crucial flash of insight may come from an unexpected source in chaotic space. Keep your eyes and ears open....

the big difference

So what does living in chaotic space look like?

Chaotic space is about the randomness of life. It is about experiencing the experience as it happens, rather than having the experience with an eye to the next one. It's like taking photographs of a place as opposed to just being in it. When you want to capture a moment on holiday, or at any time, as soon as you get the camera out you are starting to frame the moment. That in itself is not necessarily unproductive or unenjoyable. What it prevents you doing is experiencing whatever you are doing as itself. You have started to experience it with a purpose.

Knowing yourself is about understanding the defining moments in life when you were content; they may have been really small things, or very momentary. In understanding them, you open a little more of the Pandora's box that is self.

Is it that moment when you are looking out over the sea as the sun is setting and you can't help but smile?

Is it when hot apple pie and cream explode in your mouth?

Is it hearing the first few bars of a tune that moves you?

Do these qualify as nothing? If they do, what is something?

All of these are physical sensations and are also associated with a previously felt emotion. What will have been a moment for you will not be the same for me; even if we pick the same thing, it will be important for a different reason. It is the reason that you need to connect with, so you can use it to help understand what really gives you pleasure. Most of these moments will be found in chaotic space. They will be at times when you have let go voluntarily or involuntarily. They are unlikely to be things that you have planned.

So worrying so much about knowing what will happen is likely to get in the way of feeling good in a relaxed way. We may feel a sense of achievement, but that is not the same thing. That is a conditional happiness, based on you behaving in a particular way, so that you get the happiness you "deserve".

Chaotic space is about things that happen to you that make you feel good.

They can't happen to you if you are intent on seeing only what you control.

"There's a destiny that shapes our ends, rough hew them how we may......"

Shakespeare

But it isn't about being fatalistic. It is about consciously deciding to experience opportunities, both comfortable and uncomfortable.

It is not possible to know in advance how something will feel.

You can guess, assume, anticipate, but you can't know. And you certainly can't have the experience before you have had the experience.

You need to subvert the form every once in a while to get new ideas in the system, or even to have a new experience.

You can only subvert the form with something new. Something you don't know.

You don't know what you don't know…

That's right, that risky stuff again. No guarantees.

"One must still have chaos to be able to give birth to a dancing star."

Nietzsche

So in chaotic space all sorts of things happen randomly that impact on you. It isn't the "things" that happen, it's how you use, apply and live them that is the real impact. They come into your life, you decide or choose what you do with them.

What is out there that can make a difference?

Plotbreakers such as illness, accidents, traumas, successes are great places to look for pointers to our underlying values. They make everything before or since difficult to integrate, as they call into question so much of what went before. They are even capable of changing a mental model. If it happened once, it could happen again. You don't necessarily have to wait to be tapped on the shoulder by a large blunt dramatic incident before you change course. You could make the change yourself…Ponder on that radical thought.

Adrian put his hands deeper in his pockets and quickened his pace. The sun was shining and people were smiling at him. He began to feel his shoulders drop and his jaw relax. No rush, no pressure, breathe…

Adrian was 30, a bright software engineer with an exciting job in a successful dot.com company in London. He was well paid, had plenty of friends, and for no reason other than he felt like it, he decided to go travelling. He said he literally woke up one morning and felt he wanted to drift for a while.

If you were to dig deeper, you would find that while he enjoyed his job and his social life, he felt as though there was something missing. He could not put his finger on what "it" was, just that "it" made him feel restless.

Instead of going to work, he went online and bought a round-the-world air ticket. By the time he had pressed the submit button he was feeling more energy than he had felt in a while. He resigned from work and within a couple of weeks left for Nepal.

He was two months into a trip to New Zealand when one of the guys he had been travelling with was killed in a diving accident. They had been together at the time of the accident and Adrian was responsible for bringing his friend's body out of the water, and organizing contact with the family and authorities.

Adrian was not known among his friends in London for spontaneous displays of emotion, but the incident left him feeling vulnerable, and his initial response was emotional, but after a while he began to respond with a shrug of the shoulders, well that's life, attitude. A month after the incident, he continued his travels in South East Asia, trekking in remote regions.

He finally returned to London, a year after he had left, but found it difficult to settle. He had the offer of several jobs, a home to go to, and friends who were pleased to see him home. Even allowing for the post-travel depression syndrome, he was disoriented.

There are many complex dynamics here. Adrian had discovered a joy in a more permanent residence in chaotic space which was hard to reconcile with work as he had known it, and as it was presented to him. He had also experienced a major loss, in a traumatic incident. The death of his friend was not his fault, but like many people who are present at similar incidents, he was left for some time with a feeling of guilt; not only about surviving but about whether there was anything more he could have done.

"Why can't I just travel? If I take a journey, why does it always have to be going somewhere that I have dictated? Why can't I just travel and enjoy the journey?

"I feel exactly the same about everything, or at least I think I do. Since I have come back from travelling, people say I am more openly emotional. I don't remember how I was before. I don't know surprises me but doesn't scare me.

However, when I try to think about what I like and don't like, I draw a blank. I have got so used to living in the moment with my life that it's almost impossible to imagine a future. I feel as though I am waiting for the next thing to happen. I am not sure I can start anything for fear it might be thwarted or taken away. I don't think I have the ability to choose any more."

living in chaotic space

the big difference

momentum

Adrian had not accepted the lure of chaotic space. The traumatic death of his friend had made him yearn for some structure in his life.

He had not accepted random events to the extent that they could totally change his view on life. While it made him yearn for structure and safety, it also made him want to make the best out of every moment and every experience, in case he didn't get another chance.

His desire to live in the moment was a reflection of a fear that someone could take the moment away at any time. He wanted the randomness and "freedom" and excitement of chaotic space, but he wanted it in a safe framework where nothing "bad" would happen.

This is a dramatic story, but the principles are fundamental. The questions it raises are about how we deal with major life events, and the effect they have on our ability to make choices. While we have strong in-built values that we want to satisfy, they are sometimes temporarily overridden by life events. This doesn't necessarily mean that our fundamental desires have changed; it means we are responding to the moment.

Desire for conditional chaotic space is not an acceptance. Freedom means an acceptance of the random, whatever that might be.

That is a huge step. Even if you have the courage to take it once, you will still be surprised by its effect. It is at the surprise moment that your choice point first appears. The readiness to see it as potentially positive, without being Pollyanna-like about it, is part of the acceptance of the chaos.

Time to exhale again

In this chaotic world, not only are the events random, so are the behaviours of the people around you.

Sometimes this can feel harder to deal with than random events. We like to feel we know what people will do in given situations as we frequently reference ourselves through others. So if we do not feel comfortable with them, we are not comfortable with ourselves. The feelings this engenders are varied and multiple; for example, envy, embarrassment, inadequacy. They all have at least one thing in common – if you had no expectation, you wouldn't experience those feelings.

Not only do we want others to behave in a familiar way, we also seek out those who will guide and lead. Particularly in times of change, we look for those who will show us direction. Again, not necessarily a "bad" thing to do. If it stops you doing what you would rather be doing, then the question "so why do it?" arises. In a chaotic universe, as we struggle for some sort of order, we usually look outside of ourselves, whether to the universe itself to provide some construction or to someone in that universe who will either show us the way or tell us the way. There are many people out there whose own way through the chaotic universe is to tell others what to do and how to do it (sometimes avoiding having to do "it" themselves).

The Van Morrison "no guru, no method, no teacher" idea is really about trusting yourself in chaotic space. The randomness allows you to be much freer than in a structured, ordered universe.

If there are no rules, you can't break any.

One way to avoid this is not to reference through others; on an extreme scale, that usually involves ascetic, hermit-like behaviour. The power to be who and what you want to be lies in the awareness of when you need the support and guidance of others and when you know the answers yourself. This information rarely comes in a flash of lightning; it usually takes many attempts, and there are no rules. Learning to trust yourself is a lifetime process, as is trusting others. Expecting to know the right thing to do every time is going to lead to disappointment. Approach chaotic space for what it is – try out different approaches and observe their impact.

"I've been sort of dead in a way. I cut myself off from other people and become shut up in myself. And I can see that you become dead in a way when you do this. You have to live in the world *with* other people. If you don't, something dies inside. It sounds silly. I don't really understand it, but something like that seems to happen. It's funny."

R.D. Laing, case study

Relating to others is not the same as being dependent on them. A dependence on others to "fix" you stops you creating momentum because you have asked another to push you. That means they control your momentum.

It's like sitting on a swing; sometimes you need the incentive to push hard enough to make it swing; it is so much easier when someone pushes you, but that doesn't mean you can't gain the momentum by yourself. A dependency on others to drive us means that we hand over power to others, and diminish our own value. Even looking to other people, however much we love them or they love us, can thwart us; because another person, just like ourselves, is to some extent unreliable. Self-reliance is helpful, but not always reliable, and consider the pressure we would place on ourselves if we always expected ourselves to be "in". We need to know when is the time to approach someone else, and when it is only self that can make a difference.

The virtues of vague: senna pods for the soul

Within chaotic space, lines are often less clearly drawn. A less narrow focus is necessary to deal with the randomness. For those people who have big perfectionist and planning streaks, this creates major anxiety. If we do it more or less than we should, how does that impact on our relationships, and our ability to live contentedly in the world?

A narrow focus on life doesn't help us to live. It means that anything that was not accounted or planned for throws us, and we do not know how to cope. We get angry, confused, upset and depressed when things do not go as we want them to. Having those feelings isn't such a bad thing, but who wants a life dominated by them?

Staying tight is quite often our reaction to feeling incapable. We are taught at school to conform, or try harder. We perceive that giving a tight-lipped smile, or saying nothing, or planning what to say instead of listening, gets us through our contact with others. We repeat this behaviour until it is so ingrained that we believe it is who we are, and it is the only way to react.

Keith Johnstone, when teaching theater skills, used a list of "Things my teachers stopped me from doing" as a syllabus.

He had been urged to concentrate on one thing at a time, so he looked for ways of splitting the attention.

He had been taught to look ahead, so he invented games that would make it difficult to think past the next word.

Copying had been called cheating, so he made people imitate each other.

Originality and concentration had been prized, so he became famous as the acting coach who shouted, "Be more obvious!" and "Be more boring!" and "Don't concentrate!". Johnstone's mantra for being a good improviser on stage is "Don't be prepared". It's a good mantra for being in your world and allowing yourself to see possibilities. But it's hard to do when you have to have it all focused, goal-oriented and prepared.

Trying harder, one of society's mantras, puts an enormous amount of pressure on individuals. Trying harder to do what? How hard is harder? When we are pushed into trying harder, we distort both our bodies and minds with tension. Tension has the tendency to make us miserable. If we tensed ourselves further and felt even more miserable, would we learn anything? Would we do it quicker? Would we have more ideas?

Trying harder generally means "treating the mind as though it were constipated and had to have ideas squeezed out of it".

Gurdijeff called our pressure for dealing with pressure our "chief feature". Do you struggle harder or withdraw? Do you strive for more perfection or for more attention? Do you evade or dominate?

Discovering what your behaviours are under pressure is difficult because the very thing you are seeking to find is also your means of searching for it.

The distortion in the way we think distorts your efforts to correct the distortion. Trying harder increases the pressure.

"Trying harder can't make you spontaneous; it's like trying to slam a revolving door!......Trying makes you mediocre. It's like running up the down escalator."

Keith Johnstone

I can almost hear you say, "but if I don't try, I won't get anywhere". Where does that notion come from? Can you remember times in your life when you really didn't **TRY** and just let yourself do it..... .? We usually go into heavy "try" mode when we don't trust ourselves. What is that lack of trust based on, and what would happen if we let go?

When you watch any sportsman, artist or expert "trying", you usually think there is something wrong. Many will tell you that their best work has been done when they were distracted by things physical or mental. Being average allows automatic processes to take over, and there are many parts of our brain that are actually more talented than our socially adjusted selves. Our view of the world is governed by the way others see us, but our need to please others is going to get in the way of knowing what **WE** want. Living in chaotic space with all its random variables is part of the way we learn to free ourselves to be who we are, not what we think others want us to be. You can move with fluidity only within boundaries. They should support, not block.

Even chaotic space has boundaries.

When you think you will or might fail, you become stuck and either you can't move or you jump at the first thing that presents itself as a way out.

We often hold on to muscles to take away pain. When you release muscles that are chronically tense, the pain often returns. This can be true of the mind: when we hold on to things so as not to feel the pain they caused, and then we get in touch with them again, we feel the pain. However, because it is a different time…

It takes so much energy to hold things back.

"It takes a lot of work to keep an especially tight squeeze on those emotional sphincters."

Robert Sapolsky

It's a scary world out there, and it looks way more inviting to be relaxing on Paradise Island in your hammock. But if the villa is surrounded by the wall that you have built to keep out the ever-changing, mean world, you may well be exhausted from holding it at bay.

Disaster is unavoidable. Go through it, not around it. Live it, don't avoid it.

We know intellectually that this makes sense, and yet we still fight pitifully as though we could make an impact, and set ourselves up to fail. If we expect to be able to conquer all, we are certainly doomed to fail, even by the logical law of averages.

Why is it so hard to accept this? We seem to have trouble living in grey. We either opt to be masters of the universe, or give up control to "destiny". The grey would be to approach the random incidents of life as they come and trust that we will have the capacity to deal with them ourselves or know who to ask for guidance. Sounds simple enough, yet we insist on having a plan!

Or in a couple of variations we employ what Lizzie Comber refers to as the "Irish tidy up" syndrome: that is, stuff everything in the cupboard and keep your hand on it in case it falls out, but whatever you do, don't make a decision about whether what is in the cupboard is important or not. Or even whether it needs to be there… just stop it tumbling out.

Nicolette has a slightly different approach to sifting the data that she allows in her head. She is "brain bulimic"; that is, she takes in everything she can; she voraciously seeks knowledge, counsel and experience at every available opportunity. Then she feels as though it is not good for her to have all that knowledge so she dismisses it as waste and discharges it, either by denigrating it or the person who told her, or saying it is irrelevant, or incorrect, or that it doesn't apply to her.

Anyway she chooses she gets rid of it and therefore is devoid of nourishment, and goes seeking the next binge. She can however say that she has asked the questions and is therefore "dealing" with whatever her issues are.

Both of these approaches are means of temporary control. Neither attempts to deal with the fear, or really acknowledge it is there.

"You miss 100 per cent of the shots you didn't take."

Wayne Gretsky

Setting free the bears

Michael Rabiger describes improvization as "a translation of our unconsciously stored experience into action". It happens best under some special pressure and when we choose to risk trusting it. Some actors and artists fascinate us with their talent for "improvization". What matters here is their capacity to adapt, to make something good out of a chance situation, and enjoy doing so.

Everybody has this talent, but it seems to happen only when we choose to risk trusting it. The choosing is the key word. It is a conscious decision which allows us not only to let go but to capitalize on what happens as a result. If this was unconscious we would not have realized we had any opportunities.

The optimal conditions seem to be you being confronted by a situation that is risky, and there is a possibility of you failing. You may be desperate, or feeling devil may care, but either way, you plunge into the situation without any thinking. Even in the nanosecond in which you make the subconscious decision, you know if you stop to think, you're finished. So you don't go with the moment and let your "intuitive autopilot" take control.

Stanislavsky explained that it is crucial to focus on the moment, on the actual, and never on the self as it performs. If you focus on the self, you become self-conscious, and self-judging. The more you expose and relax yourself, the more you develop trust in your ability to create and act in the moment.

Living in chaotic space and changing demands our ability to not go the safe and tried path, the one of least resistance.

"We almost never think of the present, and when we do, it is only to see what light it throws on our plans for the future."

Pascal

Never up, never in

Most of the time, the present is virtually non-existent for us – we are so consumed by using the past to plan what comes next, a moment away or in the future.

How hard is it to be there? Being still and just observing what is going on around you is so difficult. It takes enormous effort to just be there. Try it. See how long you can listen to yourself being and what is going on around you. Listen to everything; cars going by, your breathing, the fridge switching on and off…..I would be surprised if you can do that for longer than two minutes; usually after about a minute, we begin to think. Our interest in just being with reality is very low. We want to think through all of our preoccupations and figure out life. So before you know it, you have forgotten about this moment, and have drifted off into your house, personal relationships, children, boss etc. Nothing wrong with it except in doing that we have lost something else. The something else is the ability to be in our reality.

We do this most of the time…..and we do it because, well, usually we are trying to protect ourselves from something. We spend a whole lot of time defending ourselves against something that has either already happened or we are actually powerless to stop.

When we are defending, we have no concept of reality,

because the defence blocks it. In fact, it frequently is denying reality's existence because if we deny its existence we don't have to do anything about it.

There is nothing wrong with considering current problems and/or planning ahead. However, when we are upset or stressed about an issue, we don't just plan, we obsess. Not knowing what to do sends us into an even more anxious state. If this continues over a period of time, we often become physically or mentally depressed. If our mind is refusing to take care of a situation, then our body takes over. At this point, we catch a cold, get skin rashes or recurrences of old viruses. It is unlikely that we could ever stop this happening completely, as sometimes our worry is so strong that it blocks everything and it takes a body shock for us to recognize what is going on. (Also, our defences can be so strong that we think we can carry on through something and if we focus hard enough, it – i.e. the worry – will go away.)

Never underestimate our feelings of omnipotence

We do so on a regular basis, but our bodies have more sense of reality than we do. So logically, in order to deal with issues, it makes more sense to be aware and in your body than out of it.

"Wherever you go, there you are."

Jon Kabat Zinn

Being aware is unlikely to have negative results, and yet we avoid it like the plague. It doesn't matter if you can't do it all the time; that would be way too hard. Just to be able to do it occasionally would help immensely. It does appear to be difficult for us to accept changes that are not something we do **ALL** the time. That is an enormous and unreal amount of pressure to place on a person.

Actually having the insight can make a huge difference.

Susie bounced into the room, her eyes sparkling. Her bullying husband had left her two months previously. "I have so much energy, but much less mess to deal with. At least when I was with Peter, I knew how he was going to behave, even though it was unpleasant. Now my relationships are all surprises. I don't know what to expect. I also can choose what I want to do. I can go on holiday where I want, wear what I want, see the films I want to. I have no one to blame at work when things go wrong. It's what I always said I wanted. Now I have it, now what? What do I do? It's hard being grown up."

So what is there in life that is stable and can be counted on?

Charlotte Beck suggests there is only one thing you can rely on:
Life being as it is.

Why is that so hard for us to accept? We don't actually want to hear it. We feel that if we believe that, then we have no control.

This is true.

What is so awful about that?

The biggest risk you can take is to count on life being as it is. Yet it is. And therefore it is low risk as it is a given.

Phew.

Being in the moment is not about doing nothing, it is about seeing what is, and then thinking about what you would choose to do. You cannot choose without having been in the moment, in the reality of what is. If you become obsessed or overwhelmed with a thought, you cannot see or know what it is. This is not about awareness of self, it is about obsession and stress.

Give it a label

So what should we be doing on the odd occasion when we let reality in? One helpful thing would be to label the thought. By labelling it, we are admitting its existence and therefore allowing ourselves to do something with it. Labelling might look like, "having a thought; she is very bossy", "having a thought, he is being unfair to me". If the thoughts are tumbling out so fast that you can't recognize anything except confusion, label the mess "confusion".
If you take away the belief that you have been wronged, the feeling goes with it. If you take away the feeling that you have been injured or hurt, the injury and hurt disappear.

Even an acceptance in this way is very liberating; you no longer have the need to expend tremendous amounts of energy holding something back, or concealing it. By surfacing it and speaking it, you can also get perspective on it; whether it is something that is worthy of your attention and is really fearful, or whether it isn't worth holding on to and you can let it go. "She is impossible" and "having a thought, she is impossible" are two very different ways of looking at the world. One judges and makes the problem external, the other owns a thought and makes it a thought, not a judgement.

Easy, huh?

Well, not really. However, the more you do it, the more we become used to ourselves and how we work our lives. If we find that certain thoughts come up hundreds of times, then we know something about ourselves we didn't know before. Perhaps we think incessantly about the past or the future. Some people always think about events, others think only about people. Some people think only about themselves. Some people's thoughts are totally focused on the judgements of others.

Getting to know ourselves takes a lifetime;

after all, we have been around for a while, and have accumulated a concomitant number of experiences and responses.

Often the ideas we have off the top of our head seem trivial and/or ridiculous. The important thing is to start. Some place, any place. Then you can play with, refine or deface the idea until it becomes something you can see might happen. There needs to be raw material, however far-fetched, that sparks energy. In general, having the freedom to feel you can say something, anything, is a huge part of being there. How often have you kicked yourself for not saying something at a particular moment, or for being tongue-tied because you couldn't formulate a statement, when it might have been better to say something rather than let the moment pass?

"When you stop taking chances, you stay where you sit
You won't live any longer, but it will feel like it."

U2

Of course, let's not get extreme about this; there are times when you can lose the momentum by saying the wrong thing. However, flagging to yourself and others by saying something at the appropriate moment is important. It doesn't have to be profound or meaningful, just a marker that identifies that moment for you. The spluttering and stuttering tend to come from those moments where we feel we have to say something mindblowing rather than a simple, "Well, that creates all kinds of thoughts for me...."

Living in and making the most of chaotic space and life's randomness means trusting yourself to be able to live through it. It means being aware that random events happen, and it is in their very randomness that we discover the freedom to be in the moment, and the importance of that experience in doing what we would rather be doing.

Awareness requires taking on the risk of being wrong or looking foolish.

Happiness requires a willingness to be unhappy.

Confidence is the courage to face a danger.

Collaboration helps and acts as reassurance for you to push yourself and move forward safely.

Freedom and power require a willingness to acknowledge that they exist and that you are prepared to accept the consequences of both freedom and power.

"Sometimes it takes darkness and the sweet
confinement of your aloneness
to learn
anything or anyone
that does not bring you alive
is too small for you."

David Whyte

CONTROL MEANS

LETTING GO.

"I obey only my own instincts and intuition. I know nothing in advance. Often I put down things which I do not understand myself, secure in the knowledge that later they will become clear and meaningful to me. I have faith in the man who is writing, who is myself, the writer."

Henry Miller

the big difference

living in chaotic space

f8 and be there

"IN THIS WORLD THERE ARE TWO TRAGEDIES:
ONE IS NOT GETTING WHAT YOU WANT;
THE OTHER IS GETTING IT."

Oscar Wilde

f8 and be there

"We make the future. We make it in our personal lives. With those we live with, we make it in our families. With our co-workers, we make it in our company or other enterprise. With our fellow citizens we determine the future of our country. And with all of our other fellow humans on this planet, we decide by what we do what the future of spaceship earth will be. In the end, we all determine the future.

"How can we depend on one another without expecting to be taken care of? When is it wise to trust the other, with what, and how much? What is the best way for each of us to manage our unmanageable lives?

"This is a powerful idea, because what it suggests is that if enough people adapt a common image of a possible future, they will all change their behaviour in ways that are consistent with that image . . . and that is largely what will evolve. At an operable level, all futures are self-fulfilling futures. If enough of us change our minds, we will change the future."

Lawrence Wilkinson

Be there

F8 is a camera aperture speed. A photographer, Ulli Michel, was asked how he managed not only to take such great photos but also to be in the right place at the right time. He replied that it was a matter of "F8 and be there". He meant he always had his aperture open, and was looking everywhere he went. That way he was always "there". This is a great metaphor for understanding how you can make "the big difference". Doing it means being there. Being open to whatever is there. Having your "aperture" permanently open. The awareness is all. Take the photograph and work it out later. Focus on what is happening rather than what has already happened or is about to happen.

"It is harder to see than to express."

Robert Henri

"Now voyager sail thou forth to seek and find."

Walt Whitman

So, the long journey **OUT**, the Big Difference; doing what you'd rather be doing. It's clear to you now what you want, where that comes from, what might get in your way; (if you have read this book in a linear fashion…)

Now what? All you have to do is do it. Why do you need another section to help you think through doing it?

If I remain true to the comments I have made previously, this chapter should be superfluous. As soon as you know what you want, the way forward becomes like a lighted aisle in an airplane. Yes, and….

Sometimes getting started down that road demands one more push. Roads are for journeys, not destinations.

"You can hold yourself back from the sufferings of the world, this is something you are free to do and is in accord with your nature, but perhaps precisely this holding back is the only suffering you may be able to avoid."

Franz Kafka

Self-realization without self-actualization is pointless. Well, so Laura Guyer Miller suggests. I wonder. Sometimes the realization leaves us so overwhelmed with what we want to do that we are paralyzed by the thought of doing something. Worse still, trying something, it not working and feeling worse than when we started. Whenever we feel as though there is something better we could be doing with our lives, we have problems trying to raise what that something might be. This puts tremendous pressure on us to find the elusive "something". Could there really be a something? Or might it be a series of somethings? How would we know?

Having chosen what you would rather be doing, understood what is behind your thinking, how do you begin to make it happen? What things help? What things get in the way? Action before the thought processes that have been described in previous sections is unlikely to get results of any worth.

"A plan is just a list of things waiting to happen."

Way of the Gun

So if you have opened this section to find out what to do, get used to disappointment. Reading the end of the story before knowing who and how the story unfolded is often an empty experience. Besides, in the case of doing the things that are important to you, there are no finite endings…

"Every new beginning comes from some other beginning's end."

Semisonic

You know of course that this changing stuff may be highly overrated. Be careful what you wish for if you want answers and change… doing what you would rather be doing is rarely a once-in-a-lifetime happening. It feels more like a potholed road with fascinating scenery to experience, if you can take your mind off tripping down a pothole and not mind if you do. A lot of "ifs".

If. Little word, big implications. A bit like big. Notice how often it creeps into your conversation.

Being there means suspending "if". It means being "if".

If means being aware enough to see opportunities. It means not being so narrow or inflexible that you cannot take the opportunities. The hints are there. We don't always take them; usually because we don't see them…

"How many times it thundered before Franklin took the hint? How many apples fell on Newton's head before he took the hint? Nature is always hinting at us."

Robert Frost

Very little happens because someone sets out to accomplish a specific goal; that is, it is rare in life to have choices in which the consequences of your actions are clear. There are usually ifs attached to goals. That doesn't mean that you don't decide what you want, it means you don't insist on it appearing in a particular package, tied up in a particular way. It also doesn't mean being uncommitted or waiting for it to happen.

By remaining uncommitted, people think they are keeping their options open; this is a plot in itself.

Re-inventing yourself does not give you the freedom from responsibilities you have created.

Even when you have taken the plunge and started off down the road, cut yourself some slack. Whenever you try something new, you have become de-skilled. You are frequently awkward and clumsy. You are likely to make mistakes.

At this point it is so easy to throw in the towel and with a huge sigh of relief go back to how it was. This is particularly true under pressure. It is also worth remembering that people have framed their world around you, and if you start to move in a different direction to the one they were expecting, you may well confuse them and consequently put them on the defensive.

This probably won't make them encouraging or tolerant of anything new you are trying. It may just be worth explaining yourself, and be more aware of their reactions to you. Learning takes time. You need it. Expect to spend it rather than expect to get it right first or second time.

"If you manage to do something
following your instinct as closely as possible,
then you have succeeded;
but that's truly exceptional.
It very rarely happens."

Francis Bacon

f 8 and be there

the big difference

momentum

The interminable everydayness of being...

Feeling alone, helpless and afraid is merely the ordinary state of affairs. Remembering this helps, but not a lot...No creature is able to control their own life. Humans are unusual in that they can be aware of this. While some mammals appear happy to stay warm, dry and fed, we worry about whether or not the moment will last, compare the moment to others we have known, or ask what really is the meaning of life. These are some of the reasons why humans get ulcers, and zebras don't.

Our consciousness makes it possible to imagine that things could be different from the way they are. Our memories and assumptions can keep us in the same place. Seeing how things might be allows us to improve our world. In doing so, we give up accepting the moment with good grace. Instead, we are drawn to intensifying and prolonging the experience and the feeling, and making it happen on a regular basis.

We spend our time preoccupied. While we are involved in this constant internal dialogue, we miss what is happening. We are not there. The shutter is not open. The senses receive the information, but because of our preoccupation, we don't do anything with the data. We are looking to solve, as we perceive that to solve means to act. The myth is that the more we have done, the better we have done.

A great deal of the fear is in the anticipation as opposed to the doing; sometimes by the time we get round to doing, we have gotten over the worst. Frequently the anticipation of doing something is far worse than the actual experience.

The fear contained in the anticipation can often talk us out of what we want to do. The other side to this is we pretend we fear nothing and just go straight to doing, to feel better. No satisfaction there...

f8 and be there

the big difference

momentum

So what do all these wise words mean?

They mean that it is hard to move on, to make the Big Difference.
Not impossible, just hard. You need to want it, not feel you need it.
At some point, you are going to have to make a leap of faith in order
to know anything further about yourself.
It's great when you experience it, trust me, I'm a writer.....

"Only those who will risk going too far can possibly find out how
far one can go."

T.S. Eliot

But seriously, if you feel you know what the Big Difference might be
in your life, you want to make it happen. You want to move from
ideation to action; let's see what that opens up.

Great myths and suspicions about making a difference

We suspect that openness augurs uncertainty.

We suspect that acceptance means acquiescence.

We believe that letting go means giving up or quitting.

These myths reflect the paradox of control. The only way to stay in control is to let go.

Let go. We often hold on to ourselves so tightly that we feel we might fall apart if we let go. We feel much lighter on our feet when we let go of our bodies; we can move faster. Ever seen a cat moving fast when it is holding on to itself? If you tense yourself, emotionally and physically, how can you move?

Forcing anything or anyone to do anything rarely had creative and exciting results. **Ideas and learning come from letting go, not holding on.**

"Don't just do something; sit there."

Thich Nhat Hanh

In order to move, we have to first yield, empty, and then push forward. Pushing before yielding and emptying results in pain and blockage.

The Miotto motto

Y   Yield

E   Empty

P   Push

Michelle Miotto suggests that unless you yield your body, the energy cannot flow. Try it. Stand up and breathe in. Breathe out and feel your shoulders drop. You may even be able to feel how tense you are. Be conscious of it and then give in to it. Feel the weight of your body moving from your muscles to your bones (that is, from a place where they are tense to the place that was meant to hold your weight). Don't fight it. Yield on your life's push. You only begin to feel what is when you yield. As you begin to yield you feel the resistance that is part of you. You need to feel the resistance before you can empty it.

Yield.

Yield and accept what is.

You cannot learn something new until you have emptied yourself. There is a famous story about a Zen master who was visited by a professor who wanted to learn about Zen. The master served the tea. He poured his visitor's cup full, and then kept on pouring. The professor watched the overflow until he could bear it no longer. "It is overfull. No more will go in." "Like this cup," the master said, "you are full of your own opinions and speculations. How can I show you Zen unless you first empty your cup?"

Our cup is usually filled to the brim with the "obvious," "common sense" and the "self-evident".

Yield is about accepting possibilities.

Think about it.

Don't keep pouring.

Try not to just rush to the next paragraph. Let the implications sink in.

Yield.

"In a beginner's mind there are many possibilities, but in the expert's there are few."

Shunryu Suzuki

We consider ourselves experts on ourselves, and in doing so, block out many possibilities. So emptying is a necessity before we can do anything new. You cannot empty until you yield.

"When they think they know the answers,
people are difficult to guide.
When they know that they don't know,
People can find their own way."

Tao Te Ching

The "don't know" mind is important to being there. If you "know" a place or a person, you pass through it or by them without looking. If a situation is new or unusual you have to be in a "don't know" state about it before you can understand it, otherwise you will assume you know it.

If you think you know, you miss the photo opportunity.

So, what does yield look like? Try this exercise to see how willing you are to yield.

Try counting to five without thinking of anything, and as soon as you think of something, go back to one. If you can actually do it, try counting to ten. It is an extraordinarily hard thing to do, particularly when you are being challenged by a person to do something. That should be a clue as to things that might stop you emptying: doing things in response to a challenge, or force, makes it hard for you to let go. You already have a competitive aim and expectation in your head. That is not empty.

Back to one. This is a hard thing to do. Because you can't do it immediately, don't give up. Many people take years to be able to count to ten in this way. It doesn't mean you can't start your journey. This is part of it.

Being there is a long-term rather than a short term commitment. Even committing to being there is a step on the road. Knowing that you can't do it overnight should be a relief, not a pressure. Yielding means being more aware of what you do and what your environment does. If you have a plan in mind, you see things in terms of that plan, not as they are.

Back to one.

The more you try to stop your thoughts intruding, the more you do. To free yourself from the need to get results, you need to know what the "one" is for you. If you don't know where you are, or what is important, you have no way of knowing how you are doing in getting there. You have to yield and empty before you can move on. To start by trying to make things happen is meaningless. Forcing yourself to stay in a place where you are not yet ready to stay is also not helpful.

Instead you need to learn to acknowledge and notice the desire to stray and be distracted, without coercion or blame…back to one.

Heading straight for a list of actions to do will give you at best a list of things you have done but no sense of achievement. Hence the emptiness many stressed people describe, and yet they are busy all the time…

They are not empty, they are actually full. Their Zen cup is overflowing. They cannot take any more in; yet the cup is so busy overflowing that they can't drink from it. So they think their lives are full, but they cannot drink from their overflowing cup (even if it's a travel mug). The ability to let something go, to yield and thence to empty, is essential to growing.

New skin does not flourish until the old has been sloughed off.

Empty

Empty is not ignorant. It is open to new. Questions are more important in this state than answers.

As a child we question things in the world that don't make sense. Why do I have to grow up? Where has the sun gone? Where do I come from? These questions are so hard for grown-ups to answer that they laugh or smile and avoid the subject. In many ways growing up is about suspending questions and getting on with the business of conforming in the world. The questioning doesn't go away. It manifests itself again when we are dissatisfied with life, or feeling lost or disappointed. We want to return to the questioning, but we don't know how, or who we can ask.

We can of course use questions to distract, divert and avoid. They can create circumstances where we are unable to commit to anything. We can't seem to put aside concerns and doubts.

How often have you slept on something to discover that the solution has appeared to you in the night? Sleep allows your "don't know mind" to come to the fore; usually when you are not thinking about things.

How will you know what you can't see? You'll know it when you can't see it.

"We live long enough to fall apart."

Robert Sapolsky

Stay uncertain, because uncertainty is the only thing that has the solid feel of truth.

f8 and be there

the big difference

momentum

Nothing is certain except that nothing is certain. Uncertainty is readiness.

It is only a problem when underneath lies a desire for a secure outcome. No outcome is ever sufficient.

So what does this mean I actually do? I hear you ask desperately.

Observing, Listening and Questioning are not passive things to do. They are doing things.

"But since humans are a part of nature, what happens in the future is only partially a result of present actions. On the one hand, humans cannot expect the future to go the way they wish just because they try to guide it........ .

"This appreciation would make change and instability seem a more 'natural' human condition because humans would not see themselves as isolated from nature – that is, conquering, or overcoming, or breaking through it."

Don Michael

If you haven't emptied, not only is there no room for you to move but there can be nothing new to engage or push. When you have accepted, been open to possibilities, you see and feel them. You can then push forward, letting go of what you no longer need.

Push forward.

Push is not force. It is your power to make you happen.

The timing of when you can move forward, even when you have yielded and are empty, is pretty important. Not only would it be hard to do, but it would probably not even be a consideration to think about change when you are having a Sylvia Plath moment.

What do you want to keep?

What do you need to lose?

What do you need to do differently?

The challenge in making things happen for you is to do them in a way that is congruous with you; sometimes this creates a conflict between what you know and are familiar with, and the risks of the new. The chances of anything changing if you go with the way you have always done it are minimal, or at best short term but unsustainable over any period of time. To create difference, not only do you have to be thinking differently, you also have to operate in a different way. Chances are thinking differently will by its very nature create a different way of doing. Sometimes, when confronted with pressure or difficulty, we revert to familiar ways of both thinking and doing, and then, guess what, nothing changes.

Knowing you may fail and accepting that is part of the choice process.

There are no recipes, but some frameworks are helpful.

YIELD

EMPTY

PUSH

"IT WOULD BE EASIER IF IT WERE

AND IT IS NOT."

EASIER.

Judy Sorum Brown

Let's take some time to blink

When confronted with the confusion of stress and/or choice, do you blink rapidly and flood your mind with thoughts in the hope that something will surface, or do you stop blinking altogether and withdraw? Either way, you are not being there.

Walter Murch in his book on filmmaking called *In the Blink of an Eye* describes blinking as a way in which we make sense of the visible discontinuities of our perceptions.

"Look at that lamp across the room. Now look back at me. Look back at the lamp. Now look back at me again. Do you see what you did? You *blinked*. Those are *cuts*. After the first look, you know that there's no reason to pan continuously from me to the lamp because you know what is in between. Your mind cut the scene. First you behold the lamp. *Cut.* Then you behold me."

John Huston

We must do this countless times in small instances, like the one John Huston describes, and also in the greater scheme of things. What do we miss with the short cut? If anything? Does it allow us to compare the two bits, the lamp and the face, without irrelevant information getting in the way? Sometimes looking from one side of the room or from one person to another can create quite a different picture…..Sometimes, when we are stressed or angry, we hold on to a single thought in the mistaken belief that doing that will keep us focused and somehow save us from whatever we fear that has made us stressed or angry. That holding on to a thought sometimes translates into not blinking, both metaphorically and literally. By the same token, when we are confronted by many conflicting emotions and thoughts, we blink desperately in the hope that it will sort things out for us, and get us back in control of ourselves.

Murch's contention is that the blink will occur where a cut in a film would have happened, as a blink denotes an internal mental separation of thought. He suggests that we watch consciously and subconsciously in others for blinking as an indication that an idea has been presented, that the person has understood what we are saying, and/or gets that the blink denotes something of significance.

(Watch Keanu Reeves in the film *My Private Idaho*. In one scene around a campfire, he doesn't stop blinking, while River Phoenix is talking about himself hardly blinking at all. Is he distracted, trying too hard, watching something we can't see? He certainly doesn't appear to be in the moment.)

So being conscious of a blink moment may help you identify difficult thought points for you.

Be clear about what you are working with: You

It is very reassuring to be clear about what your dilemmas are. If we oversimplify what the issues are, we put ourselves under tremendous pressure. To say "well, it's only a matter of" begs the question about why you have done nothing thus far if it's that simple. As the rest of the book demonstrates, underpinning most problems and solutions are complex dilemmas that have to be managed.

What is it you are doing and thinking?

Diagnosing in a concrete way how you are acting and responding, without generalizing, is very helpful. For example, saying I always need to be in control is too overarching a statement. What does that mean you actually do? Boss people about? Get obsessive? Shout a lot? Telling and not asking?

Looking at what you are actually doing and thinking helps to consider how you might change it for a more effective outcome. Check what is creating that way of thinking or doing.

Blink

The cumulative power of your actions helps build momentum. With momentum, you add energy and force to the next result you want to create. Without momentum, you start over with each new situation. Knowing your pattern is part of building momentum.

If we return to the screenplay metaphor, what would your new one look like? Now that you know what the old movie was like, are you up for directing and starring in your next one?

Where do I start?

Blink.

A poem…….

"begins as a lump in the throat, a sense of wrong, a homesickness, a lovesickness. It is never a thought to begin with."

Robert Frost

This is the closest I get to a plan, but it means a script outline, and probably only a beginning. Just to encourage and reassure you that you are on a road, and it is not one you have travelled before. So

fear not if the scenery is unfamiliar,

or there are people in it you don't know. Both should be true, for you to be moving on.

It is about choosing a framework and the kinds of action and characters you want to be around. It isn't about scripting your or their words or actions (more of a Mike Leigh film than a *Die Hard* episode).

In life, I believe that…

I will show this in action through…..

The main conflict is between…

The main point of view/character will be…

Who are the characters you want to be around? How do you want to be and how do you want to relate to them? What kind of action or interaction do you want to experience? What scene-setting or background exposition would you make?

"TOMORROW IS PROMISED TO

NO ONE."

William Goldman

EXPECT THE UNEXPECTED.

ACCEPT WITHOUT BLAME.

IF YOUR CAMERA APERTURE IS NOT OPEN, IT'S HARD TO KNOW WHAT IS GOING ON AROUND YOU.

IF YOU DON'T GET CURIOUS AND ASK THE QUESTIONS, NOTHING GETS INSPIRED OR CLARIFIED.

ACCEPT THE IMPERFECT.

ACCEPT.

KEEP IT OPEN. BE THERE.

STAY CURIOUS. ASK.

GO THERE.

f 8 and be there

the big difference

momentum

"HOW FAR IS ALL THE WAY, AND THEN IF IT STOPS, WHAT'S STOPPING IT, AND WHAT'S BEHIND WHAT'S STOPPING IT? SO WHAT'S THE END, YOU KNOW, THAT'S MY QUESTION TO YOU."

David in *Spinal Tap*